About the Author

Juliet M. Dujmovic is a certified life coach helping young women build their confidence and the lives they desire through her practice *Let's Get Your Life Together.* From her own experience of getting married, she also recognises the need for and specialises in bridal coaching.

Aussie grown and London settled (currently… things change); Juliet is on her own journey of personal development, continuously learning and getting the most out of every day, one day at a time.

What They Don't Tell You About
Planning Your Own Wedding

Juliet M. Dujmovic

What They Don't Tell You About
Planning Your Own Wedding

Dear Adam,
All the best and happy
reading!

Juliet M. Dujmovic

Olympia Publishers
London

www.olympiapublishers.com
OLYMPIA PAPERBACK EDITION

A CIP catalogue record for this title is
available from the British Library.

ISBN: 978-1-78830-738-3

First Published in 2020

Olympia Publishers
Tallis House
2 Tallis Street
London
EC4Y 0AB

Printed in Great Britain

Dedication

To my mum and dad, Rosie and Joe, for always believing I can do it and never doubting my abilities to do anything I set my mind to.

And to my husband, Luke, for without him, there would be no story to tell.

Acknowledgements

Thank you to the women I sought feedback from for different sections of this book—Abbie, Ratna and especially Marissa. To my Zia, for always being ready to make time for me and for reading my book through in one sitting. To my family, both new and old, for allowing me to write this story truthfully. A big thank you to my mum and dad, who instilled in me the hardworking skills I needed to write this book, and for so confidently knowing that I could do this. Your faith in me never wavered, and I love you both very much. Finally, a very special thank you to my husband, Luke, who supported me both financially and emotionally, who never doubted his confidence in me or my endeavours, and who read and edited my book not once but twice through. In so many ways this book is your baby too, because you helped me make it possible. I love you with absolutely all of my heart.

Contents

Introduction

I tapped Mum on the shoulder and cleared my throat. She turned around; I was looking at my hand so she followed my gaze, and when she saw the ring, she shouted, "Bullshit!"

I've never seen my mum so happy in my life. She was glowing and smiling so hard I couldn't see her eyeballs.

It was between Christmas and New Year's Eve 2016 when my now-husband Luke popped the question. Even though we had spoken about getting married plenty of times already, when the moment came and he got down on one knee, he was still nervous and I was still surprised. I even shocked myself and cried a little bit.

We were in Brisbane, Australia on holidays with all of our parents and siblings, but Luke and I had decided to go out to dinner just the two of us, and it was this night that he proposed. After our dinner, we met our family at the restaurant where they were, and it was at this moment that I tapped Mum on the shoulder. Once everyone else had realised what had happened, we all started celebrating together. We proceeded to ring our grandparents and extended family back in our hometown Adelaide, Australia, and there were shrieks and tears and laughter. We were the first of our generation to get married, and everyone was incredibly excited.

A few days later, once the buzz had subsided and the ring was comfortably settling into its new home on my finger, reality hit and I realised just how busier life was about to become…

All of a sudden, we had this huge party to organise. I thought to myself, yeah, I got this. How hard could it be?

There are so many different working parts to a wedding: the venue, the ceremony, dresses, DJs, cakes, a budget to worry about, people to organise. I kept on discovering new things to add to the list as we went along. To date, this was the biggest event I have ever had to organise. I would have a guess that, for the average bride and groom, this would be true for others too. Heck, it might even be the biggest event of your entire life that you have to plan.

The thing that I learnt is, a wedding is not just a party. A wedding is the beginning of a marriage, and it represents so much more than just a party. Not only is there the planning of the event, there is an additional layer of emotion to the entire day. And not just for the couple getting married—it is emotional for the parents, the grandparents, brothers and sisters, any kids involved, aunties or uncles, friends... you get the picture. It is an emotional day for all the people close to you. But I did not really know or anticipate this beforehand. I literally had NO IDEA what kind of emotions were going to be coming along for the wedding ride… feelings of happiness, excitement, nervousness, stress, anxiety, overwhelm, guilt, tension…

So, when I say be prepared for emotions, I mean be prepared for both positive and negative emotions. *Of course* I was expecting the positive ones. I will be marrying the love of my life, and through this wedding we would be creating the start of our new family together. This was an incredibly exciting thought and I was happy to be doing so with Luke. We would also be planning a beautiful wedding, and the organising queen in me was channelling Monica from *Friends* and was getting scarily excited. And lastly, this would be a party to look forward to. For any wedding, let alone my own, I would look forward to dressing up, having a couple of drinks and letting my hair down a bit. The same was going to stand for our own wedding. So yes, I was feeling these positive emotions of happiness, excitement and good times. But I was not expecting any of the *other* emotions. Nor did I have any idea about the INTENSITY of emotion I would feel. Being the first to get married in my immediate family and friends, I had not been a bridesmaid before and I had not been married before. I had never been that heavily involved in a wedding (I have been a flower girl twice, but they don't really count here as I don't remember much!). All I knew of weddings was what I had seen when attending one as a guest. So, I was going into my own wedding pretty unaware of what goes on behind the scenes of planning a wedding.

Spoiler alert—pressures and pains do exist when it comes to planning a wedding; we just don't really talk about it.

"How DARE such a wonderful day be tainted with anything negative!"

"It is the best day of your life; how could you feel anything but positive emotions!!"

Shame on anyone who projects this on a bride if they are trying to speak up about their feelings about their wedding day. Feelings can be complicated, but feelings are feelings. If someone is feeling something, who is anyone to tell them otherwise? However, a bit of a catch-22 goes on when it comes to negative feelings about your own wedding: no one talks about the negative emotions, so the less you hear about them. And no one hears about the negative emotions, so no one talks about them for fear of being shut down for 'dampening' such a wonderful day. "Bottle it up and pretend they don't exist," said no therapist ever.

You know where we do get an idea of what big white weddings are like? The media. They are always a great help when it comes to truly representing reality. In the weddings we see on the TV, in movies, in magazines, we get either the glorified white fairytale-esque weddings, or we get the bridezilla weddings. It is one end of the wedding spectrum or the other. The fairytale-esque weddings show only the beautiful side of weddings. They are like the Instagram account of 'weddings'; you get the highlight reel. You do not get the full picture. The bridezilla kind use this Bridezilla character as a mocking representation of all the pressure that is put on the bride, and now she is a monster who has cracked and exploded. Having been a bride now, I do understand where Bridezilla has come from. I can very easily see how the pressure on the bride can lead her to crack. But crack in multiple ways too, not just your stereotypical hot-tempered, snappy bride. But instead of making a mockery of the exploded bride, why has no one given attention to the step before the bride cracks, and address the pressure on her???

From all around us, we do not actually get a real representation of what planning a wedding is like. If you take the media lightly, then ok, sure, it is just entertainment. But when that is the only experience of wedding planning that you see, the real thing can come as a bit of a shock when you realise just how much work is involved, the relationships that either make it through or break, and all the emotions that you experience. My poor mum wiped away my tears on a few occasions leading up to our wedding. They were almost always stress tears. And you know when you get to the point where you start feeling bad about feeling bad about something that you are supposed to be feeling good about? That is where I got. I felt guilty for having these feelings about my own wedding, which made everything worse. Why did I feel this guilt? Because I did not know it was normal to feel like this about my own wedding. No one talks about it!

I tried researching how I could deal with what I was going through. At that point in my life I had not really discovered self-development, so I didn't really know about self-care or taking care of my mental health. I approached this in the way that I knew how to at the time, and that was the practical approach of researching. I tried finding studies on weddings (the scientist in me) to work out if what I was feeling was normal, and what was out there that could help me, if anything. I found lots on marriage, but very little information specifically on weddings. And trust, I do know how to research. From the little that I could find on weddings, I did find a standout potential reason as to why there is so little research out there on the big white wedding. Chrys Ingraham wrote in her book *White Weddings: Romancing Heterosexuality in Popular Culture* that it could be because heterosexuality is so highly organised by Western society and culture that so much depends on it, and it is too sacred and too close to home to scrutinise[1]. Where marriage is legal, same-sex weddings are exempt from this because they are relatively new in human history, and they don't quite have to adhere to the same rules as heterosexual weddings. In many ways they are creating the rules as they go. But heterosexual weddings have a very solid,

---

[1] Ingraham, C. 1999, *White Weddings: Romancing Heterosexuality in popular culture*, Routledge, NY.

long history with the big white wedding. Who wants to rock *that* big boat?

Because of the little research we have on weddings, we have a lot of traditions that stand which we don't really know the meaning of anymore, and we don't have a true representation of what to really expect when planning a wedding. Some of us don't even know what to expect of the wedding itself. I feel more and more, especially if you are from the millennial generation and younger, that we are brought up to question things a lot more than previous generations, which stirs the pot but, for the purpose of greater understanding, is completely warranted. We have also been unpacking the mental health box more and more these days, and female empowerment is being ever revitalised in all arenas. But when it comes to weddings, there are lots of gaps and not a lot of answers, answers that as a bride I found I was looking for. Now I want to help other brides.

This is why I am writing this book.

Firstly, I want to share my wedding planning experience with you so you can get some idea of what to expect. I don't for one second believe my experience is isolated. I got on with the wedding planning and survived just fine, but not without lessons learnt. For anything new we undertake, we are bound to make mistakes, discover things as we go along, and find more things to add to the to-do list. This is how we grow and learn, but it can still be very overwhelming. Every bit of this applies to the planning of your own wedding, and we can all learn from each other's experiences. Hopefully, *my* wedding planning story can help you prepare for *your* wedding planning story, and let you know you are not alone in your experience.

Secondly, I want to coach you through your own wedding. In hindsight, I wish I had known who I could have reached out to for some external support during this time in my life. Someone who I could have talked to about all the emotions I was going through and all the actions I needed to take. You see, the people I typically turn to, the ones I am closest with, were all *involved* in the wedding. Sometimes I felt I needed to talk to someone removed from the wedding, because I did not want to offend anyone or have someone take something the wrong way. At the time, I also didn't know anyone who had recently been married, who I was comfortable enough to talk with about their experience and see if what I was going through was normal.

Knowing what I know now—writing this book several years on from my wedding—what I wanted was essentially a life coach. Someone who could have, quite literally, coached me through the wedding planning process. Someone who could have listened unbiased to all the emotions I wanted to let out, and guide me to find out how I was going to deal with them. Someone who would also be able to listen as I talked about the practical bits of the wedding and create a plan of attack on how I was going to get things done. Someone who would guide me into finding out more about *how* I was going to solve my problems, reduce the overwhelming number of tasks into small bite-sized steps, and keep me checked in with that action. So, in this book, I have provided you with self-coaching questions and exercises to guide you through your own wedding planning journey, and hopefully it will make the process just that little bit easier for you.

To all the brides out there, who might be questioning a detail in their wedding, who are panicking and are feeling bad about something, or who are freaking out about planning such a huge event, this book is for you. It is also for the brides who have no idea what to expect, and do not want to be blind-sided. While so far, I have only really talked about my white heterosexual wedding experience, this book is appropriate for any wedding, be it same-sex, heterosexual, of different cultures or religions, or gender fluid. It will not matter who you are or what kind of wedding you are having; this book focuses on the PROCESS of planning, as opposed to the wedding itself. My experience is obviously *my* experience, it is factual now and part of my past, so while I will use my story to illustrate a point, you can take that point and apply it to your own experience. And that goes for 'bride' as well: bride can be whatever gender you want it to be!

Who am I?

I am going to pause here and take this point to briefly tell you a little bit about myself.

My name is Juliet and I am a born and bred Australian. I have lived in 3 countries; Australia, New Zealand and the UK. At the time of writing I currently reside in London. My time in London has been an incredible experience filled with all the ups and downs involved with moving half way across the world. The main one is—and as clichéd as it sounds—it has been a very big personal development journey of getting to know myself. It was during this time of my life where I properly discovered self-development, including self-care and mental health care. This was not really my intention; it was just a happy accident. But one thing has led to another and I have found myself in a career that I am in love with: life coaching. I am a certified life coach with a Diploma in Personal Performance Coaching, with my own coaching business called Let's Get Your Life Together. I coach women who are in their 20s and 30s—female millennials. Within that group of women, are brides-to-be.

I called my business Let's Get Your Life Together because

coaching is a relationship. 'Let's' is short for 'let us', i.e., Let *us* Get Your Life Together. In coaching, we are equals and you take action on your goals with me by your side. You may have full responsibility and ownership of your goals, but you are not alone. I do like using the word 'let's'. So, as a heads up for this book, whenever I say 'let's…' the meaning intended is 'let us do this together'. Life is more fun when we're in it together!

As you may have gathered from the opening lines of this book, I myself am married and have had the big white wedding. I met my husband Luke at 18 years of age on our last day of school: 11th of November 2011 (that's 11/11/11—remember this!). Five years later, he proposed, and on the 11th of November 2017 (see it?) we got married in Adelaide, Australia. Our engagement was just under 11 months long, which is a relatively short engagement, so the entire wedding planning process was quite condensed for us. What made our wedding unique was the fact that Luke, the groom, was living in New Zealand for the majority of our engagement, leaving most of the wedding preparations to me. Needless to say, I have first-hand experience of what planning a wedding is like, and a busy one at that!

Since my wedding, I have been a bridesmaid once so far. I am currently at the age where everyone around me is becoming engaged, and I am constantly having conversations with brides-to-be. But I am also part of a huge Italian family that migrated to Australia post-war. The thing about being part of a large family is that I have been a guest to many weddings. I have attended at least 2 weddings in each year of my short life. That would total something like 50 weddings in my memorable life time. All of these weddings have been in Australia, and they include weddings from all sorts of backgrounds and nationalities, both family and friends who have been close to me and more distant. Saying that, they have all mostly fallen into that Western-style heterosexual wedding category. But, overall, weddings have been a constant presence in my life.

I am combining my knowledge and passion for being a life coach with my experience of weddings and wedding planning, to strive to be the best bridal coach out there for brides-to-be. My experience of getting married is still fresh and relatable, and I am writing it to you, as one bride to another. Because there is so little research on weddings available, in my head there is an urgency to get something out there to fill that void. Something on what to expect about weddings, to help as many brides-to-be as possible. That is my book's purpose.

If you have any questions or comments about anything you read in this book, you are more than welcome to contact me through Let's Get Your Life Together's website and social media. I would love to hear from other brides about their raw experiences of planning their wedding. Who knows, maybe in 10 years' time I will upgrade the book to include some of your experiences.

Ok, so I've mentioned life coaching a few times now. I am a life coach, and this is partly a coaching book for your wedding planning process. Life coaching is a pretty broad term though, so let's get on the same page as to what life coaching is.

What is Life Coaching?

In my wise hindsight, as I said earlier, I know that what I wanted during my wedding planning process was a life coach. I know this because I myself am now a trained life coach. I know what life coaching is and what the differences are between therapy, mentoring and life coaching. I can confidently say it was a coach that I wanted, because I had a GOAL. There was an outcome I wanted to work towards: the goal of our successful wedding day. I needed an action plan to get all the tasks completed, and I had dates and deadlines I needed to stick to. I also needed to increase my self-awareness to work out what was holding me back and causing me anxiety on some things, and what was exciting me on others. I needed to work out how to deal with the emotions I was experiencing, how to balance wedding planning with the rest of my life commitments, and how to work with others, professionally and within my family. I was after SOLUTIONS. And, all encompassing, I wanted to work it out myself. I did not want to give our wedding day to a wedding planner and let them take all that organising fun away from me. I wanted to be part of it. This way I would feel proud of myself and feel the responsibility of our wedding planning.

This is what life coaching gives.

One of the leading figures in the industry, Sir John Whitmore, defines life coaching in his book *Coaching for Performance* as **'unlocking people's potential to maximise their own performance'**. It is about helping you raise your awareness, help you discover what is important to you, and draw out your potential, all within the context of your end goal. Goals can be all shapes and sizes. They can be as small as finding half an hour a day to relax in your busy schedule, or as big as building a business. Because life coaching focusses on the PROCESS of moving closer to your goal, it is versatile and can suit many goals. If you are reading this book, your end goal would be your wedding. Other words for 'goal' you could use might be your dream, your aim, your target—whichever word you prefer. For the purposes of this book, I'm going to use the word goal, and we can easily break a wedding goal down into medium- and short-term goals.

Most people are not brought up to be self-reflective, and for others this is not something that comes naturally. But for those who wish to improve themselves and how they perform, life coaching could be something that ties your personal development with your wedding. Some tasks just need more exploring, to help you understand emotions behind any resistance you are putting up, and a life coach can help you dissect this in a removed and unbiased way. Others might also need some external help to keep them accountable to themselves and get tasks done. This is what life coaching does. In a broader sense, life coaching, in the school I have been trained in, believes that everything you need to achieve your goals is there inside you already; it is just a matter of helping you increase your self-awareness so that you can see this in yourself, for yourself. As a result, life coaches don't advise you; that's the realm of a mentor. By discovering the answers for yourself, you will find your own meaning in what you are doing, and when you find this, you are more likely to achieve your goals.

Coaching is a very practical approach to wedding planning, and completely revolves around TAKING ACTION. To me, this is the difference between therapy and coaching, and why I know now that it was the latter that I wanted when I was a bride-to-be. Both deal with talking about issues, but coaching focuses on the 'how' we are going to solve it, more so than the 'why' the problem exists in the first place. Coaching is more future-focused, whereas therapy focuses more on unpacking past events. It is important to know the difference between different professions, so that you can better judge which help is more appropriate for your issue at hand. For you, it may very well be that mentoring or therapy is better suited for your needs, and that is absolutely fine; we are all different and so are our needs. But I am still happy you are reading this book and I hope you find value in it regardless.

How this Book is Structured

As well as the introduction and conclusion, this book is divided into 7 Chapters:

1. Practical Bits
2. Communication
3. Mental Health
4. Money
5. Family Politics
6. Traditions and Generations
7. Post-Wedding

These, I have found, are 7 main areas that are general enough to cover most types of weddings, but are so important to the smooth-sailing process of planning your wedding. For you, there may be more categories, there may be less. The point of this book is to help you in *your* wedding planning process. So, as with any book, these are the words and experiences of me, the author, and you do not have to agree with everything I write here. Take the bits that resonate and are useful to you, and discard the other bits.

A lot of the chapters are closely related. Communication is a key feature for the success of your wedding planning, so will feature strongly in the other chapters too. Throughout the book, I have mentioned communicating with 'key players' a lot. Key players refer to your partner, your parents, your in-laws, your wedding coordinator, your wedding vendors or suppliers... essentially anyone who is relevant in the planning of your wedding and needs to know some information. I have used the term 'key players' as a shortcut instead of listing all these potential people. You will know who your key players are.

Each chapter begins with a brief introduction to the chapter, followed by a <u>Your Story Brain Dump Space</u>. This is a space for you to brain dump all the details for YOUR wedding story, relative to that chapter. These can be lists, ideas, drawings, dot points, anything on your to-do list for your wedding so far. They can also be problems or issues you are facing in the topic of that particular chapter. It will be most beneficial for you to brain dump in this space (or even somewhere else that has more room) BEFORE reading each chapter, so that you are not influenced by the chapter content itself. After you have finished brain dumping, proceed with the chapter reading, and if the story or the questions you read spur on an idea or a thought, you can add to this brain dump space or note your idea in your own journaling space.

Then follows the <u>My Story</u> section. You will notice I have interspersed the text here with <u>Your Story</u> sections filled with coaching-style questions. These questions are the building blocks to help you build your own wedding plan, relative to that chapter topic. I recommend writing down your answers to each question as you go along, in a journal, on your laptop, or any other means you prefer for recording your answers. You will also notice a <u>Suggestion Box</u>. This <u>Suggestion Box</u> is not life coaching; this is me with a mentor hat on, giving you evidence-based advice from my experience, one bride to another. Wedding planning is quite practical and task-based, so I think there is a lot you can learn from other people's experiences. It may be of use to you, in which case I am happy to share my story and suggestions.

The first four chapters will each contain a section called

Bonus Material. Here I will place any spreadsheets, templates, coaching exercises, and anything else that I found useful for my own wedding and wish to make available to you. If you head to www.letsgetyourlifetogether.com/bridalcoaching, you will find all the bonus material in free digital format for you to download.

All the chapters bar the last finish with a Further Reading section where, if you would like to read more on that chapter topic, I have recommended a couple of books and articles, including any referenced material from that chapter.

Throughout all the text, you will also find little tips, indicated by the obviously-titled 'TIP'. An accumulative list of these TIPs can be found at the end of the book in Appendix A.

Before we get into all of that though, we have a disclaimer section on you, my dear, the bride.

What Kind of Bride are You?

We live in a society that loves to label everything and everyone; labels make it easier to organise the world. But, unfortunately, human life is too dynamic for that, so I am not going to use labels. Humans do, however, have TENDENCIES. For example, I know I *tend* to prefer organisation in my life, and I love to make lists and work through them. But I am only like this when I want to be. There are times when I am happy with some beautiful chaos and would rather just go with the flow, without a plan. I am sure you can think of similar tendencies in your life.

So, when it comes to your own wedding, you are probably going to have a few tendencies too. These tendencies might lead to some *assumptions* as to what kind of bride you are. Technically this section's title is misleading, because we aren't going to answer that question as there aren't any bride categories guys! There are only tendencies!! I tricked you!!!

Have a look at the sentence over the page, and think about how you would fill in the blanks. Below this sentence there is a list with a handful of options for the blanks. This list is by no means exhaustive—you can use other words or phrases you can think of.

How you fill in this sentence will change from day to day throughout your wedding planning journey. You, your thoughts, and your feelings, are all dynamic. They are constantly changing, and no two days will this sentence feel the same. That is totally OK.

```
┌─────────────────────────────────────────────┐
│                                             │
│  I TEND TO _____,        │
│                                             │
│      BUT SOMETIMES I CAN                    │
│                                             │
│      _____.            │
│                                             │
└─────────────────────────────────────────────┘
```

Procrastinate

Be proactive

Walk away from problems

Be a problem-solver

Get things done

Panic when under pressure

Just want my own space

Be short-tempered

Cry

Write lists

Go with the flow

Anger easily

Avoid responsibility

Take control

Share

Hog a task for myself

Be a team player

Deal with pressure well

Get flustered

Prefer to work on my own

Enjoy speaking to people

See tasks clearly

Be level-headed

Be organised

Forget things

Enjoy planning

Attract people

Shy away from confrontation

Be calm

Explain things well

Be the one who people come to talk to

Be there for others

Practical Bits

Planning your wedding is essentially planning a big event. It has some very practical, tangible things you need to do, so let's start with these practical bits. This chapter is basically a guide to creating your wedding plan and how to keep organised and on top of everything.

Practical bits quite literally refer to every practical bit about the wedding:
- Booking the ceremony
- Booking a venue
- Booking a photographer, videographer, caterer (if venue doesn't provide), etc.
- Hiring equipment or backdrops, if desired
- Ordering the cake
- Choosing the dress, the bridesmaid dresses, the suits
- Ordering invites
- Etc.

There are PLENTY of these practical bits. These are essentially all the things on your wedding to-do list. This is the list of things that can be really daunting and overwhelming when you think about them all at the same time. But you do not have to *DO* them all at the same time, so let's break down that list into smaller chunks to chew, and make everything more manageable.

Your Story Brain Dump Space

My Story

I am an ORGANISING QUEEN. I get way too much satisfaction out of organising things, be it my desk or a room or an event. It could even just be a drawer and I will get excited. I am secure enough in myself to claim that I am pretty darn good at it. This part of my wedding was probably the most natural for me, so I knew I would not be needing a wedding planner. I hope you can definitely take something away from my story here.

YOUR STORY BUILDING BLOCK #1: ORGANISATION SKILLS

> *What are your organising skills like?*
> *If you were to rate your organising skills on a scale from 1 to 10, with 1 being 'really poor' and 10 being 'organising queen', where would you be?*
> *How do you feel about organising a wedding?*
> *What is scaring you the most?*
> *What are you most excited about?*
> *Who could you speak to, to make the wedding planning process easier?*

Organising Tools

When starting a project, it can be helpful to set up some organising tools that will help keep you organised. The type of organising tools that will best help you will depend on how best you learn.

> Are you a **visual** person, someone who likes to see things?
> Do you prefer learning by **physical** means, by physically touching and experiencing something?

Are you someone who prefers **aural** learning, someone who has 'a good ear'?

Knowing which learning style you prefer to learn with will help you decide on which organising tools will best suit you. There are several other learning styles than those listed above, but I will focus on these 3 means—visual, physical and aural—as these are the most common amongst people. Below are a few examples of tools you could use for each of the learning styles to give you a few ideas:

VISUAL	PHYSICAL	AURAL
A wall planner Digital note-taking A to-scale drawing of a timeline	A physical notebook/diary and pen Sticky notes A box full of notes, samples, leaflets, etc.	Alarms and digital reminders Voice memos Repeating text out loud

I am very much a visual and physical person. For our wedding, I used the following tools in the ways described. I have also indicated which learning style the tool most relates to.

NOTEBOOK (physical)

The first thing I did when starting to plan was, I got a giant A4 wedding notebook. The one I chose was divided into 3 sections; one section was lined paper, one section was graph paper, and the third section was blank paper. It even had a little pouch at the back to put business cards and other bits in. All my wedding notes, all the suppliers' and vendors' business cards, all bits of ribbon samples, all went in this book. I used the lined paper for writing, I used the graph paper for rough money costs and budgeting, and I used the blank paper for drawing seating plan layouts or invitation designs. This helped to keep everything wedding related all in the same place, and for all our meetings, I'd just grab this book and go.

SPREADSHEET (visual)

The second piece of organisation I created was a Microsoft Excel spreadsheet for tracking everything money related. In the notebook, which came with me to every single meeting, I wrote rough costs and prices; in the Excel spreadsheet, I recorded EVERYTHING. I used one of the wedding budgeting templates provided in Excel, and customised that to suit our wedding. There will be more detail about this spreadsheet in the Money chapter.

A BOX (physical)

The third part of my little organisation set was a box. It was just an A4 size box that I repurposed around the house, nothing fancy. Here I put all the bigger loose items that did not fit into my notebook pouch, like invitation samples. Again, this just helped to make sure everything was in the same place, and I did not lose any important bits of paper, such as invoices. An alternative to a box could also have been a binder folder. This would have worked just as well.

A DIGITAL FOLDER (visual)

Between spreadsheets, quotes and emails, there were a lot of digital files. I saved them all in one place in a digital folder on my desktop called "Wedding". In hindsight, I could even have created a folder in my email and saved all the wedding related emails there, because I can assure you there will be A LOT OF EMAILS. Dealing with emails is made easier now that we can just search for key words in our email search bar, but having them all in one folder would have made it just that bit easier again.

I kept this folder nice and organised too, with sub-files called 'Food', 'Guest Lists', 'Invitations', 'Church', etc. Simple short titles that were instantly recognisable. When I had received a quote or an artwork proof, some of them came with titles made up of numbers and letters, the likes of '43845744urej784.doc'. I resaved these all with an appropriate title and a date as soon as I received them, something along the lines of 'CakeQuote_TheCakeShop_15May17.doc'. This way it was obvious what documents were what, and it made it easier to navigate through the files, especially as the number of them grew. I dated them because, on more than one occasion, we needed to request multiple quotes from the same place, so the dates told me which the most recent ones were.

A PHYSICAL DIARY (physical)

Lastly, but most definitely not least, is a diary. This is probably the most typical tool for organising, be it a physical diary, a digital calendar, a wall planner, etc.; whichever one you most prefer. At the very basic level, a diary helps you organise and divide your time across all of your commitments. I have never had so many personal appointments and meetings in my life as I did during our wedding planning year. I needed to have a diary on me at all times; I was having phone calls everywhere and needed to jot down times and dates all the time. I had to note dates that I was free as well as the dates that other people were free, and try to coordinate these to ensure that when meetings were arranged, all key players were available. Without this diary, there was no way I could have remembered all the commitments I had. A diary also came in useful for writing in and keeping track of all the deadlines for payments and orders. Maybe because our engagement was only 11 months, and 4 of those I myself was in New Zealand with Luke, wedding planning seemed very busy; I would say we were having on average *at least* one appointment or meeting per fortnight when in Adelaide, so my diary was my best friend during this time. I wouldn't say we had a simple wedding, so you very well may not have as many appointments as we did. Big wedding or small, a means of recording your wedding appointments will be necessary.

In addition to the organisation tools above, I made good friends with a few stationery items. A pen was always at hand with my notebook, but also sticky tape and a stapler were really useful for sticking samples into my notebook and stapling receipts to quotes once paid for.

YOUR STORY BUILDING BLOCK #2: ORGANISATION TOOLS

> *How do you like to approach a project?*
> *What means of learning do you prefer: visual, physical, aural, or any other style?*
> *What tools do you want to set up to help you for your wedding planning?*
> *What works well for you when it comes to organising?*
> *What does NOT work well?*
> *What have you done in the past that you have successfully organised?*
> *What did you learn from that experience?*
> *How do you want to sort all your wedding-related*

things?
How do you want to record and remind yourself of all
your dates and deadlines?
What things will you need to buy?
What things will you need to prepare?
When can you set your organising tools up? Set a date!

Simple Wedding Plan

Now that you've had a think about what organisation tools will help you throughout your wedding planning journey, the next step is to tackle that wedding to-do list. You might like to refer to some of the items you dropped into your 'Your Story Brain Dump Space' earlier, or even add to it during this section.

Looking at or thinking about all of your wedding to-do tasks in one big lump will easily cause you some feelings of being overwhelmed. So let's not do that. Instead, let's start with a broad, simple plan, and then go from there. I'll show you how.

The first step to more easily digesting the wedding planning process, is to portion out the wedding into smaller parts. Using our wedding as an example, we first divided our wedding into 3 main parts:

1. The engagement party
2. The marriage ceremony
3. The wedding reception

These 3 parts formed the basic ingredients for our wedding.

From here, we broke these 3 main parts into smaller parts, aiming to have no more than 15 items in total. Our parents, Luke and I came up with:

1. The engagement party   1
2. The marriage ceremony:
   - Location   2
   - Celebrant   3
3. The wedding reception:
   - Booking a wedding venue and/or catering   4
   - The photographer and/or videographer   5
   - The DJ/band   6
   - Hair and makeup   7
   - The wedding dress   8
   - The bridesmaids' and flower girls' dresses   9
   - The groom's and groomsmen's suits   10
   - The invites   11
   - The cake   12
   - The florist   13
   - The party favours   14

These were the big key items for our wedding. The wedding was our end goal, and these big items were our **major marking posts** on the journey towards that goal. As you can see, there were 14 items, spread across an 11-month journey. This was much easier to digest—14 is doable!

The items on our list are pretty common items, so you may find this list is similar to yours. Nonetheless, our wedding was not a small wedding. If you are having a simpler wedding, you may find you have fewer items, which is even more manageable. If your wedding is bigger, that is fine too. However, the point of this step is to keep the plan simple. When your list starts to have 15-20 items or more on it, it can start to get overwhelming. So keep this list limited to 15 items or under. This will force you to think in big broad strokes. Anything else can be added in as detail later on.

YOUR STORY BUILDING BLOCK #3: MAJOR MARKING POSTS

What big key items are on your list that make up the major marking posts towards your wedding?
Who could you talk to, to find out if you've forgotten any major marking posts?

The first little step is done—how was that? Hopefully not too bad. We are now going to rank these items on your list in order of priority. The importance of prioritising here is to give your list some direction. This will help you decide which items to focus on first, and which ones can be left until later along the wedding planning journey.

If you're feeling good, continue onto the next step. If you are a bride who *tends* to not worry about the detail and just go with the flow, the next steps might not suit you, in which case do your thing. If you are currently still feeling a little daunted by the big plan, take a break and let the list you've come up with so far sit with you for a bit. It may sound strange, but just get comfortable with it and take this process at your own pace.

So, the next thing we are doing is ranking the marking posts in order of priority. How you prioritise your marking posts depends on what is most important to you. Maybe you have a particular wedding vendor you want to work with—a photographer or DJ—and you want to make sure you book them in first on a day they're free. Maybe you want a very specific date—maybe one with sentimental value—and whoever is free on that date is who you will book in. What is most important to you?

Having a short question to help guide you through the ranking process can really help keep the process focused, especially if there's more than one person working on this list. A few example guiding questions could be as follows:
- Which ones are more important?
- Which ones need to be booked in as soon as possible?
- Which ones need the most time to complete?
- Which ones need the most work to complete?

YOUR STORY BUILDING BLOCK #4: GUIDING QUESTION FOR RANKING

What might your guiding question be to help you rank your major marking posts?

For our wedding, we chose to focus on urgency. We asked ourselves, which items needed to be booked in first?

The venue:

A wedding venue is where you have the reception for your wedding. This can be a barn, a winery, a hall, a hotel, a restaurant, or your backyard—wherever you want it to be. Whichever venue you choose, it is most likely that they can only host one event at a time. Therefore, venues get booked out the quickest, and the more popular the venue the further in advance you need to book them. So, this was the most urgent big thing we needed to address.

The caterer, the photographer and/or videographer, DJ/band, hair and makeup:

Once you have one thing booked in, you will have a date that you can bring to everyone else (wedding suppliers, vendors, etc.) and see if they are free. We didn't have any particular vendors that we specifically wanted to use, so we let the availability of the wedding venue dictate the date of our wedding (and by coincidence a sentimental date was available so we ran with that). I grouped these items—caterer, photographer and/or videographer, DJ/band, hair and makeup—all together. We found, after speaking to a few, that most photographers, videographers, DJs and makeup artists were usually self-employed or a small business, which meant that they mostly could only book one wedding per day just like the venue. These then became our 2nd priority to book in because the same principle that applied to the venue applied here: because they can only book one event in per day, they are likely to be booked out faster.

You may not have to worry about booking in an external caterer. For many common wedding reception venues, they usually provide the catering. But if you have a unique venue, you may have to supply your own. This will just depend on where you end up choosing.

The celebrant, the ceremony location, the cake, the florist:

These were our 3rd priority. Cake makers and florists can typically provide for a couple of orders per day, especially the cake makers. Similarly, celebrants can perform one or two weddings in a day; or more. This meant that, as opposed to the items higher up on the priority list, these were the least likely to be booked out. The celebrant and the ceremony location are more important to book in than the cake though (probably obvious), as we found that the cake could actually be ordered quite late in the game. The celebrant usually will also have the paperwork for you to document your marriage, and these will need to be submitted by certain dates as well. For Luke and I, I knew I had to organise and plan this ahead. With Luke living in New Zealand at the time, if he was needed to sign paperwork, I had 2 options: I could send them to him by post, or take them with me on my trips to New Zealand. I did not want to use the postal option because of the importance of the documents, so I needed to make sure the documents were ready to come with me on my New Zealand trips. This might be important for you too if you have a partner overseas, or if you are actually getting married in a different state or country altogether.

The ceremony location was going to dictate how much time in advance we were going to need to book it in. If it was going to be a traditional location, like a church, this very well may be a 2-in-1 sort of deal with the celebrant, i.e., if a priest is booked in, most likely so is the church he was assigned to, and sometimes the same also applies vice versa (this is not always the case so it will depend on the religious house you use!). If it is a non-traditional location, then you would need to ensure that the location is licensed to host wedding ceremonies, and this may or may not make the booking process longer.

The florist was a pretty big one to book in too, but was not as urgent to be 1st or 2nd priority. I had no idea when it came to florists, so we spoke to people and googled the most popular ones in our area, and went around to each of them with a rough idea of what Luke and I were after. The florists themselves helped to suggest which flowers we could use, as Luke and I only really knew what colours we wanted. My mum, mother-in-law and I visited 4 places in total and got a quote from each. The quotes, quite strangely, varied in costs A LOT—some were double the prices of others!—so it was evident that allowing the time to do a bit of research paid off.

The engagement party:

The engagement party will typically coincide with the engagement itself. Therefore, the sooner this is held, the more relevant it will feel, as everyone will still be on a high from the engagement news. Not everyone has an engagement party, and that is totally fine. We chose to have one, and we chose to have a Sunday lunch at a restaurant with our immediate family and friends as we did not want anything too big. This was just another little extra thing that we needed to book in and book in early.

All the items mentioned so far have been about booking something in to ensure availability on the wedding day. The rest of the items on the list are things that need to be ordered or tasks that need to be completed, as opposed to things that need to be booked in. As a result, they weren't too high up on our priorities list. However, some of these items take a long time to complete, so work on them needed to begin early.

The wedding dress:

This is usually the biggest item that needs to be bought, and it's also usually the item that takes the longest amount of time to be completed. After doing a little research, it was recommended to us to order the dress 6 months before the wedding. This was to allow enough time for it to be made or ordered in, and to allow for any alterations that needed to happen when it came in. Therefore, wedding dress shopping needed to start early in our 11-month engagement. Other options could be to hire a dress, buy a dress online, or buy a dress in a non-wedding shop, in which case the 6-month deadline may not have been required. If you are not sure what you want, starting early will ensure that all options remain available to you.

The bridesmaids' and flower girls' dresses:

Depending on where you get your bridesmaids' dresses, you may need to order these well in advance as well. Some of the specialty bridesmaids' dress shops we went to said to order the dresses at least 3 months prior to the wedding. The same went for the flower girls' dresses if we bought them from a bridal shop. This was to ensure that, if your bridesmaids are going to all wear the same dress, you can get all the sizes you need, and also allow time for alterations. However, if you find a dress in another, less specialised shop, you might be lucky and get all the sizes you need off the rack. The trick here is being able to get all the correct sizes of the same dress. Wouldn't life just be too easy if all the right sizes were in stock on the day you happen to go in? So, I had to allow plenty of time for ordering in sizes, just in case.

If you're not doing the same dress-style thing for your bridesmaids, and are maybe just giving your bridesmaids a guiding colour or style to go buy their own dress, then that's one less thing for you to worry about. All you need to do at this point then, is decide which way you want to go. You might not even be considering dresses, but some thought into attire will be needed. The more time you have though, the less rushed your decision will be.

The invites:

The invitations we decided needed to be sent out 6-7 weeks before the wedding. Some people choose to send 'save the date' cards months in advance, in which case this would be an additional, higher priority task to organise. Consideration needs to go into the RSVP date as well. This date needs to allow enough time for caterers, who—for our wedding at least—needed to know at least 2 weeks before the wedding date a final head count so that they would know how much food they would need to order, including catering for any dietary requirements. We decided we would make our RSVP date 3 weeks before the wedding, to allow a week of buffer to chase up any RSVPs we had not heard from (TIP: Speak to your own caterers to see how much notice they require, and then add another week on for chasing up!).

The suits:

If some of your bridal party attire involves suits, your actions here will depend on what you want to choose, whether you want them custom-made, off the rack or hiring them. This I left to Luke and his parents, and they chose to hire suits. They took advantage of the few occasions when Luke came to Adelaide throughout our engagement, and used this time to find where they would hire the suits. They found a supplier and locked in the date, type of suit (colour/cut), number of suits, accessories, etc. The suit fittings were only required a month prior to the wedding, which would allow enough time for alterations, just in case any of the men changed weight or shape. Most suiters and tailors were keen to complete alterations as last minute as possible for this very reason. The alterations would be completed with a 2-day turnaround, so this was not an issue. If the suits you choose are custom-made, you will need to allow a lot more time than 2 days. Getting that conversation with the tailor started early will help to easily plan this.

Even if you don't require suits or dresses, maybe you require some other attire that needs special requirements (cultural dress, etc). Nonetheless, the earlier in the process these conversations are started, the easier it will be to plan.

The party favours:

Party favours are kind of like the adult version of a lolly bag at a kids' party. They are a little token of thanks to give to your wedding guests to take home. These do not really have to be completed until almost the day of your wedding. But you do need to order them or make them in advance so that they are ready to go. You may choose not to have party favours, which is absolutely fine. For our wedding we decided to have them, especially as we had a sit-down meal and it was easy to put one down for each plate. In our family, guests who RSVP 'No' to a wedding will sometimes still give a wedding gift, so we thought it would be nice if we prepared a party favour for them as well, as a token of thanks. As a result, the number of party favours depended on the number of invited guests, not the number of guests who RSVPed 'Yes'. Therefore, we did not need to wait until the RSVPs were all in; we could order our party favours as soon as we had the final guest list. Once they were ordered, that was another checkbox ticked off and one less thing to worry about; we just had to store them safely. If anything in the order was forgotten or broken, we would have plenty of time to remedy the issue if we ordered them earlier rather than later. If you choose party favours that are edible, such as cookies, maybe ordering as early as possible is not an option. So, how much time in advance you can order your party favours will depend on what you actually choose for a party favour.

After considering all of the above, I could now rank the major marking posts in order of priority, with more specific instruction:

1. Book the wedding venue
2. Book the engagement party
3. Book the photographer and/or videographer
4. Book the DJ/band
5. Book the hairdresser and makeup artist
6. Book the celebrant and organise paperwork
7. Book the ceremony location
8. Book the florist
9. Order my wedding dress at least 6 months before the wedding
10. Order and send out invites 6-7 weeks before the wedding
11. Order the bridesmaids' and flower girls' dresses at least 3 months before the wedding
12. Order the cake at least 2 months before the wedding
13. Order the party favours when guest list is finalised
14. Hire and alter the groom's and groomsmen's suits

Now it's your turn. Remember your guiding question you thought about earlier, to help you rank your major marking posts? Use that question, as well as some of the thoughtful questions below, to form your own ranked list.

YOUR STORY BUILDING BLOCK #5: THOUGHTFUL QUESTIONS FOR RANKING
How do you want to rank your marking posts?

What are the most important?

What are the most urgent?

What might be something that you need to give particular focus to for your wedding?

What items can you leave until closer to the wedding date?

Now, even though I *tend* to love a good list, I am a visual person, so I drew up a timeline as well as this list. This helps make visual sense to me, since a timeline truly resembles a journey towards the end goal, the wedding day. This is what it looked like:

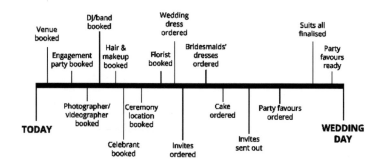

As soon as we had that venue booked in, we had a wedding date. So, on my timeline I could also add WHEN I needed to get each task done by and date the major marking posts. As such, you will notice that I wrote them all in the past tense. Not everything needed to be dated, just roughly placed where they needed to be completed by. For example, the wedding dress needed to be ordered 6 months before the wedding date. Since the venue was booked in for November 11, this task needed to be done roughly by May 11. But the invites, for example, just needed to be ordered in time to check them all and be ready to go out on Sep 17 (about 8 weeks before the wedding), so the date on which we were actually going to order them by was more flexible. This is what my final timeline looked like:

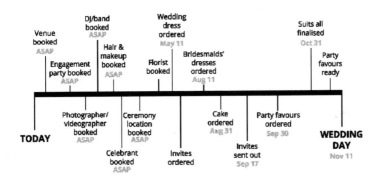

If you like this way of displaying your wedding planning journey too, then you're in luck—there's a timeline template for you in the Bonus Material section! This is a very visual way of portraying your wedding journey, so this may or may not be of use to you. Either way, if you're a little stuck on this step, you might like to use some of the questions below to help your thought process when displaying your final list of items, and deciding on dates for each.

YOUR STORY BUILDING BLOCK #6: HELPFUL QUESTIONS

How do you want to make note of your marking posts and your wedding day goal?

How will you decide on the date of the wedding day?

What happens if your choice venue/supplier isn't available that date?

What are your back up dates?

Knowing your final date, what are the deadlines for your major marking posts?
Who can you talk to, to find out about dates and deadlines for each of your marking posts?

That's it! Your simple wedding plan is complete! This little timeline, list, or however you wish to display it, is the foundation to your wedding planning journey. This forms the base guideline that you can follow along for the rest of your journey, tweaking details here and there. It is always useful to have a base, even if it is completely different from what you end up actually doing. Having a base means you have a starting point. How can you go along any journey without having a starting point?

YOUR STORY BUILDING BLOCK #7: REFLECTION QUESTIONS

How do you feel about your overall wedding plan?
Who else, other than yourself, needs to know about these dates and deadlines?

Detailed Wedding Plan

Now, if you *tend* to not fuss about the detail, and like to flow with a little plan but not much more, then you can stop with the Simple Wedding Plan. But if you are like me, and *tend* to give plenty of attention to detail, then read on. So far, you've created a broad, simple plan; now we will narrow down and look into each of the marking posts in your plan.

First, a few tips and questions to help you along and get you thinking about how you want to organise some of the detail, and where to find wedding vendors and suppliers, if you don't know any already. For the first 2 months of our engagement, both Luke and I were living in New Zealand, so our parents did the groundwork for our wedding venue and booked it in for us during this period to get it done as soon as possible. They also found a potential photographer, videographer and DJ for us through the recommendation of the venue staff. The venue had these viewing show days where you can visit the venue and meet other wedding suppliers and vendors who are displaying their goods or services on the day. When I was back in Adelaide, we attended a couple of these, as well as our local Wedding Expo, so that we could sample as many suppliers as possible in one go and get ideas. These were very useful, and as a bride-to-be I won a free photoshoot from one of these events. It is not every day you are engaged so make the most of the fiancé title!

YOUR STORY BUILDING BLOCK #8: WEDDING SHOWS

What public wedding events are accessible for you that you can attend?

Who could you speak to—staff at your wedding venue, your photographer, etc.—who might be able to recommend other wedding vendors and suppliers?

What wedding shows do the wedding vendors and suppliers display at?

Some of the suppliers and vendors we needed were easily booked in; others were not so easy. The hairdresser was easy to book because my hairdresser at the time was happy to take on the job, however, the makeup artist was trickier as I didn't know anyone. Besides myself, my 4 bridesmaids, my mum, and my aunty, were all hoping to get their makeup done at our house on the morning of our wedding. We either needed to hire 2 artists to get everyone done in time, or hire someone who was super quick and could put makeup on all of us. Some artists did not want to work with anyone else because each artist has a different style. Others were already booked in, or did not come to your house, which was a requirement we needed of them. I had to try a couple of artists out throughout the year (I had plenty of events for testing!), but on the recommendation of another artist we hired a fantastic lady who was able to get each of us done in almost half an hour and the job was fantastic. The point is, because I didn't know anyone, I needed to do a little more homework and test a couple of people out. I needed time to do this, so I got on it early.

YOUR STORY BUILDING BLOCK #9: WEDDING VENDORS AND SUPPLIERS

Which wedding vendors do you know you are definitely going to hire?

Which areas do you need to do some research in to find people?

Who could you talk to—friends, family, etc.—that can help you find people?

Who works in or near that particular industry (photography, makeup artistry, etc.) that might know someone who does weddings?

Whether you are getting married in a religious house or by a civil celebrant, there will be some paperwork to organise. TIP: Even if it doesn't have to be filled out and submitted for a long time, ensure you know what you need to fill out early, and the dates it needs to be submitted by. For our wedding, we decided to have our marriage ceremony at our local church, and that church came with the local priest. This meant that if we wanted that church, we had no choice but to have the priest who was assigned to that church. It just so happened that during our engagement, the priest at our local church was being assigned to another church interstate, and a new one had not been assigned to our church yet. It got to about May and we still did not know who the new priest was who would be marrying us. Even though I was super organised, the church was not. There was a lot of chasing up and involvement with the celebrant, and in hindsight I was glad at least that I was on top of things, or the situation could have been worse. We ran out of time for deadlines and needed Luke to sign papers quicker than he could get to Australia, so we had the extra hassle of having to pay for embassy witnesses and finding local Catholic priests in New Zealand to witness signatures. From speaking to other couples, all of this depends on the church you go to; our church just happened to be stricter and was going through a transition period. But you don't know until you know, so I'm glad I got in touch with the church early on.

Luke and I are of the same religion, so this made things a little bit easier as we only needed the one ceremony. There have been weddings that I have attended where the couple are from 2 different religions, and in order to have been recognised as married in each of their religions, they needed 2 marriage ceremonies, one in each of their religious houses. Some same-sex couples I have met needed to get married more than once to be recognised as married in different countries/states; one same-sex couple I know has 3 wedding dates (this is an unfortunate hurdle for same-sex couples at the time of writing, especially when they move from place to place). If you are requiring more than one ceremony, this will most likely translate into more paperwork, so ensure you know early what you need to fill out, when to submit by, and to where you need to submit to.

YOUR STORY BUILDING BLOCK #10: MARRIAGE CEREMONY AND CELEBRANT

What do you need to consider for your marriage ceremony and celebrant (different countries, different religions, different laws, etc.)?

How much time will you need to allow to work through the paperwork?

How many celebrants/ceremonies will you be having?

We stuck to the major marking posts along our timeline fairly well. We ordered our invitations ahead of schedule in May, even though they were going to be sent out in September, and lucky we did because there were some errors in the printing that needed to be corrected. Where I did not stick to the timeline was with the party favours. We had decided to have marble coasters with each guest's name engraved into the coaster, which would then double as the name placement for the seating arrangements. This order did not go through until October 31st, a month later than planned for on the timeline. We got the coasters in time for the wedding day, but in transit one box was majorly damaged, and a dozen or so coasters were broken. While the company happily replaced them, we had not allowed enough time for them to be delivered in time for the wedding, which meant some people did not get a coaster on the wedding day. We just explained the incident to those particular people at the reception, and that they'll receive their coaster post-wedding. They were all really understanding; things happen. Had I ordered these as per my timeline though, it would not have been an issue. And there wasn't a particular reason they were ordered late either; things just slip past your attention sometimes. It happens! The timeline helped though, because overall, I had worked out the dates that would allow the wiggle room to deal with damaged deliveries, mistakes and errors, etc. I had given myself time to address anything that popped up, including any surprise tasks that hadn't been planned for. Without the timeline, I wouldn't have known if I was early, on due course or running late, and the uncertainty would have caused me anxiety. It's that fear of not knowing. Sounds extreme, but I'm sure we've all had those moments where we were worried about an assignment, a project, our finances, only because we hadn't given any attention to it in a while and didn't really know what state it was in. But when we actually sit down and address it, we realise all is good and relax (and probably put the task off again for a while, but still, you get my point). It's that feeling of 'I have it under control'. This is the feeling a timeline, or a dated list, or whichever method you chose for your Simple Wedding Plan, gives you.

So, get on the planning early; the earlier the better. Note to all the procrastinators out there, or if you work best when you do things last minute: this style may suit you fine, but only when you work by yourself. The thing about a wedding is, it is not just you who has got things to do. A wedding is a collaboration. Each of the suppliers, vendors, venue coordinators, caterers, family members... all the key players will require different deadlines, and you, you who is 50% of the couple who all of this is for, you will need to be aware of these deadlines. They will also all have different styles of working; not everyone will be cool with your last-minute efforts. A little planning at the beginning will pay-off big time. Think of it as working now, procrastinating later. Procrastinate the procrastination!

A lot of the major marking posts listed above are pretty

straight forward; book in a makeup artist, order a cake, etc. They are almost just one step away from being complete, i.e., call the makeup artist and book them in. Done. However, some of the tasks require more detail than just that.

Remember the very first step you did, breaking down the wedding into its big main parts? Well, you can do the same thing for each of the marking posts—you break them down. This is easily done, and this will create the short-term goals for each marking post. For example:

1. For the marriage ceremony, we needed to decide on the ceremony content, the wedding songs, and hire a cellist and violinist (this was our choice; musicians are not always a requirement. Some people simply use pre-recorded music—still a task to do though. Else, no music at all!).

2. The photographer needed different locations for the wedding photos, and one of the locations we chose was an underground bar, which needed to be booked. A wedding car and a limousine also needed to be hired to transport Luke, myself and the bridal party to each of these locations throughout the day.

3. Where I have said wedding dress and bridesmaids' dresses, this also included shoes, jewellery, clutch purses, choosing a hair style…

And so on.

It is the detail for each of the marking posts that can get really messy and overwhelming, but it is also the detail that can really make the wedding. The 2 main things to keep in mind are:

---

1. One thing at a time
2. Keep it clear and simple

With these 2 things, you can't go wrong. By approaching each of your marking posts one at a time, and breaking it down into the detail one at a time, you avoid the overwhelming kind of panic. As already mentioned, some of you will be fine working with just a Simple Wedding Plan. But some of you, like myself, *tend* to prefer the attention-to-detail kind of plan. Some of you *tend* to also get quite caught up in the detail, losing sight of the bigger picture. For your wedding, don't get too hung up on making a really detailed plan. There is a certain point where you can't plan any further, or where the effort you're putting into the plan is not worth the payoff that is coming out. Some people prefer to focus on the *planning* part in a bid to avoid the *doing* part. But guys—life is not 100% plannable. As such, your wedding won't be 100% plannable. A good plan is a flexible plan, and the simpler and clearer it is, the more flexible it is also likely to be. Because unexpected things happen, and that's fine. Expect the unexpected as the saying goes. So, stick with me here, I'm going to get detailed with you on your plan, but I'm going to show you how to do so without getting overwhelmed, losing simplicity or going overboard.

I learnt this little lesson from one of my maths teachers in high school. You know how you have that one school teacher who left an impact on you? Mine was my maths teacher, and she taught me this in regards to maths, but actually I apply it EVERYWHERE (literally, I apply it even to just doing the dishes). When you are breaking down a problem, be it a maths problem, life problem, chore, whatever, break it down into the smallest parts possible. This is what I mean by simple. When you have small, simple parts, they are easier to deal with, more so than a big vague task where you don't know where to start.

Let's look at an example of breaking down one of the marking posts into its smaller short-term goals, and how we can keep it clear and simple:

Major marking post: Book the photographer.

Once we had booked our photographer in, all was not complete. I had to ask the question: What did the photographer need from us? One request was a list of a maximum of 3 x locations where our wedding photos would be taken.

Let's break that down further.

The **first short-term goal** was to choose the 3 x locations. We chose 3 x local places: a garden, a university building, and an underground bar.

The **second short-term goal** was to prepare for those places. The garden and the university building were public and we didn't need to do anything further there. The underground bar though we needed to book. To do that, we needed to make a phone call.

A phone call. That is a clear and simple task!

That took all of 5 minutes to do. This is a little plan of attack, and we broke it down and simplified it all the way down to a phone call. And that phone call I had with the bar staff only lasted something like 2 minutes. Tiny! You will also notice I did not date these tasks. Sure, the photographer needed to know our locations at the very latest 2 weeks before our wedding, but if I had left that phone call to the underground bar until within a month of the wedding, chances are they probably would've been booked out. The phone call was an initial phone call that could have happened early on whenever I had the chance, just to enquire about how much time in advance I would need to book the bar, and how much it would cost. From that phone call, we could take that information, decide yay or nay to the underground bar as a photoshoot location, and plan our next steps.

But until that phone call happened, any further planning on the photo locations would be unnecessary and somewhat useless. We had to complete the task before planning any further. The planning to be done unveiled itself in time.

There are other ways we could've achieved this too. Instead of a phone call, which maybe I was uncomfortable with, I could've sent an email. Again, a simple, clear, 5-10 min job. Maybe I preferred to visit the bar incognito one evening with friends, suss it out, and then speak to the manager in person. There is no right answer or particularly better route here, just whichever one I preferred to do. But, in any case, what you want is to narrow it down to a simple, clear action. If you're not sure if it's simple or clear enough, try breaking it down again. As an action, a phone call can't really be broken down any further. This will be a tell-tale sign of whether you have reached a simple clear task or not. Keep going until you can't break a task down any further.

Planning for the Actual Day of the Wedding

So far, I've been talking about the planning *leading up to* the wedding day. I also recommend doing a little planning for the day itself. As the bride, and as a fellow bride, we want the day to go as smoothly as possible and without ourselves, our partners, and in some cases our parents having to worry about anything. I mean, this is THE DAY, the day everyone close to us has been working towards for almost a year, sometimes more, and it is finally the time to enjoy it. After our wedding, I found out a couple of things that happened on the day that thankfully I was not aware of and other people had dealt with. Sometimes it does not matter how organised you are, things still do not go as planned. If this happens, that is ok; things are definitely going to happen, and you just need to expect that. Again, expect the unexpected. As the bride though, I did not want to be the one who had to deal with any of these unexpected things, nor did Luke. I'm sure you don't want to either. Ignorance is bliss on your wedding day. So, to avoid having to deal with things on our day, I organised in advance some tools to help the day roll out smoothly and without chaos, and we designated other people to deal with little jobs too.

The first organising thing I did in preparation for the actual day of—and this may or may not be too much for you—was write up a schedule for the morning and then another schedule for the entire day. My dad actually mentioned this in his wedding speech. Call it anal, I don't care. It worked. We had 5 women and 2 flower girls who needed their hair done, and 7 women who needed their makeup done. The hair was being done at a salon 15 minutes away, and the makeup was being done at our house. We had bridesmaids arriving at different times, and different orders being delivered, such as the flowers and the catered food ordered for the morning (TIP: Ordering some food for the morning was a really good idea, and something to think about for your own wedding. On such a big day, eating can be the first thing you forget to do, so this will ensure you are not running on an empty stomach!). We had photographers and videographers arriving at set times, and they had asked that the makeup artist do my makeup last in order to get photos of the process.

A special mention must go to my dad here, bless him, who basically was a taxi back and forth between home and the hairdresser for us ladies (this was after he had already gotten up at 5am to pick up freshly baked Nutella donut balls from our local 24/7 bakery!). The schedule I had written up told him, starting at 7am, which women he needed to take to the hairdresser and at what time, and which women he needed to return home to the makeup artist. I printed extra schedules so anyone who wanted to know where someone was could just check these. I admit, this very well could be classed as over-detailing for some people, which looks like it clashes with my earlier comments about not over-planning. The reason for this schedule was to be used as a communication tool (more on this later). It was a helpful tool to create order out of a potentially chaotic situation, only because the hair and makeup were being done in 2 different locations. Had they both been in one location, we would have saved time with the commuting (and the communicating) and the schedule probably wouldn't have been necessary. The main person who used this schedule was my dad who was taxiing us everywhere. The apple doesn't fall far from the tree sometimes; I knew this would suit my dad's style of working, because in this respect we're quite similar, and my dad appreciated this schedule. Regardless, it was a well-oiled machine that morning, so much so that we ended up finishing with about an hour to spare. We all got a chance to eat some food, relax and just soak up the moment. So, yay for my schedule! TIP: If you do create a schedule, add some buffer time to each activity. For example, did the makeup lady say she can do a face in 30 minutes? Then allow 40-45 minutes. Adding that extra 5-15 minutes to each timeslot will take the pressure off, and it will feel better when you start finishing up early, relative to the schedule. It will also allow time for toilet breaks, spontaneous phone calls, or snack breaks.

For the full day schedule, I wrote in all the deliveries: the times that the photographer was arriving at Luke's parents' house and then my parents' house, what times the florist would arrive at our houses and at the venue, and what time the cake would be delivered to the venue. I also wrote in the times that the photographer needed to leave, what time the speeches were, and what times the food courses were going to be served. All of these details were in this full day schedule. I sent this to all the suppliers and parents, and printed hardcopies just in case. The vendors and suppliers indeed needed this itinerary, but I made copies available to all the key players, so that no one would need to ask me when something was happening; they could just look at the schedule (another communicating tool—more on this later).

Onto the ceremony: it all went very smoothly. We kissed, we married, and then we went off on location for our photos. The first photos were in a garden just down the road from the church. This is where we had family photos. In order to fit all 3 locations into the time between the ceremony and the reception, we had to be on a tight schedule, and upon the request of the photographer—and this was a fantastic recommendation, so TIP this—we made a list of the order of the photos, like this:

1. Photo #1: Luke and Juliet
2. Photo #2: Luke, Juliet, and Luke's parents
3. Photo #3: Luke, Juliet, and Juliet's parents
4. Photo #4: Luke, Juliet, and siblings
5. …
6. …

We designated Luke's uncle the photo organiser and gave him this list. He shouted out who was needed for each photo and got the people for the next photo ready to go. This was genius and worked so well, and we got through all 30 photos we needed, plus a few extras successfully in the hour we had for this location.

I've been at the wedding photoshoots for other newlywed couples where there wasn't any particular organisation, and time was wasted gathering people, or people just looking around like, "Who's next?". Thankfully our photographer knew from experience how to avoid this. TIP: Speak to your wedding vendors and suppliers, as they know from experience what has and hasn't worked well in past weddings they have been part of, and may have a few tricks up their sleeves to help you with your wedding.

I like to call this next little bit of wedding day planning your Wedding Day Survival Kit. This is basically your insurance policy for any of the little things that might be required for you or your partner on the day (maybe even your bridal party). Sit down and really think about everything you might need on the day, and prepare it in a little bag beforehand. I'm talking tissues, painkillers, band-aids, spare lipsticks. For our wedding day, Luke organised an extra shirt for the wedding reception to ensure he looked fresh, because it was November in Australia and it was likely to be a warm day. In Adelaide the heat is usually dry, but we happened to get the most humid day of the year, and it was a warm 31°C, so we also brought plenty of water and snacks to load up our wedding limousine with for us and all the bridal party, to ensure no one faints on us. Check out the list of potential items that I have included in the Bonus Material section of this chapter to give you some ideas of what you could organise to build your own Wedding Day Survival Kit.

YOUR STORY BUILDING BLOCK #11: THE DAY OF PLANNING QUESTIONS

What could you prepare for your wedding day to make things go smoother?

Who can you give these items to, to take care of?
What items do you want to prepare for your wedding day?
Where or who with can you leave these items?

When it comes to all the lists, details, and notes for your wedding day—TIP: print off spares. We printed off spares of everything so that I could literally take myself out of action for the day and also ensure that if anyone forgot something, we had spares a-plenty. I printed lists for literally everyone. During the day, the florist, DJ, photographer and videographer all needed to communicate, so I made sure that everyone had a full list of each other's contact details (check out the Bonus Material section of the <u>Communication</u> chapter for a contacts list template). I printed extra copies of the readings for the marriage ceremony, and I emailed both the contact details and the readings to everyone as well, just in case they lost the hardcopy. I printed the list with the line-up of family photos for the photographer and Luke's uncle, and I printed extras. I kept all these spare sheets in a folder which sat in the Wedding Day Survival Kit. If anyone wanted to sabotage the wedding by forgetting something, they had no idea who they were dealing with—I had spares of everything. Nothing was getting in the way of this wedding while I was involved! But, let's be a little environmentally conscious here—when I say spares, I mean 1 or 2 hardcopies, and digital copies just in case someone else can go print an extra copy last second if required. And not spares with just a 2-line reading on an A4 piece of paper. For some of the shorter text spares, I printed multiple on one page, and also back-to-back. These are just emergency pages, so it's ok to print multiple items on the same piece of paper. After all, we're all in the same location on the wedding day and can indeed share.

What spare items will you need for:
The pre-ceremony preparation?
The ceremony?
Between ceremony and reception?
The reception?
The wedding photoshoot?
How will you confirm everyone's roles in the wedding day (before the day)?
How else can you reduce the responsibilities on you on your wedding day, and make your role easier?

Lastly, designated people. When it comes to designating people little jobs on the wedding day, you are going to want people you can trust and rely on. As mentioned earlier, we chose Luke's uncle as the designated person to organise the photos on location, because we knew he was close enough to us that he would be in the photos and thus present at the location, but also he understood what we were asking him to do and, most importantly, has experience successfully leading and organising people. We were assigned a wedding coordinator by the reception venue for the entire wedding planning process, and during the reception she oversaw all the catering and venue-related affairs. We brought a lockable bag for all our monetary wedding gifts, and gave this to a trusted person to take care of, who would then give it to the hotel manager to lock in their office for the night. We definitely wanted someone we trusted 100% for this job! For other weddings I have been part of, buses have been hired to transport a party of guests; sometimes people organise this for their elderly guests or weddings that are in hard to get to locations. Sometimes another guest is a designated driver, so thought will need to go into who these people will be.

YOUR STORY BUILDING BLOCK #13: DESIGNATED PEOPLE

What jobs need to be done throughout your wedding day?

Who can you designate these jobs to?

If you are currently responsible for some of these jobs, how can you give this job to someone else?

Who do you trust the most?

Who do you definitely NOT trust doing these jobs? (Rule some people out!)

When can you speak to these people and organise these jobs (before the wedding day)?

Suggestion Box

1. USE A DIARY.

You are going to need a way to remember all your appointments and meetings. If you are skilled at just using your memory to remember your schedule then that is fine you can ignore this. But I definitely recommend some form of a diary, be it buying a physical diary for this time in your life or using reminders on a digital device.

2. MAKE A PLAN EARLY AND PRIORITISE.

Sit down early and make a list of all the major things you need to do, and record all the dates for when things need to be done by. Decide what is the most urgent, what is the most important, and what is going to need a lot of time to complete. This will help you prioritise your tasks, and spread the tasks out throughout your wedding planning period. If you sit down and plan early, you are more likely to be calm and think of everything you need, instead of going at it without a plan and maybe forgetting something halfway through. Once you have a plan, then you have your starting point, you can add and tweak things as you go along, and it will not be as daunting.

3. KEEP EVERYTHING IN ONE PLACE.

You can be like me and have several places: a box, a notebook, a diary, a digital folder, or you can keep absolutely everything in just one place —for example, say, scan everything and keep it all in a digital location. Whichever way you decide is best for you, it will be a lot easier for you to find that little piece of paper with the florist's phone number on it, if you know you have at least taken photos of it or put it in that one place.

4. HANDLE THE DETAIL FOR ONE MAJOR MARKING POST AT A TIME.

Sometimes it is the little things that count. But if you think of all the details for everything in one go, then your to-do list will be so long that everything blurs and your stomach does a somersault just thinking about how much you have to do! Approach each major marking post one at a time. If it is time to think about the wedding dress, break it down into the detail: shoes, jewellery, purse, tiara maybe? Tights? Little scarf or jacket if it is winter? And then stop. Have a decent break before you attempt the detail for the next big thing. Listen to your gut here; if you are feeling overwhelmed, you've probably thought about too much in one go—breathe and take a smaller bite.

5. CHECK THE MARRIAGE DOCUMENTS YOU NEED TO ORGANISE EARLY.

This is super important if you are like us and have a partner living in a different country, or plan on getting married in a different state/country. This may also be particularly important if two different religious statuses are involved, if one or both partners have been divorced before, or if your marriage status needs to follow different laws in different states/countries. For all cases, finding out what documents are needed early on will be the best way to combat any nasty surprises down the track.

6. START CONVERSATIONS EARLY.

If you are like I was and have no idea about planning a wedding, then start conversations as early as possible. Speak to family and friends and see if they know of anyone they can recommend for different wedding services. This is how I found my hairdresser, makeup artist, florist, and wedding car. Utilising your connections through family and friends may even get you a discount. Speak to your wedding venue coordinators and suppliers to see who they have worked with in the past for photographers, videographers and DJs. These people live off of recommendations. Also have conversations with these people to gather information, to find out how much time you need to allow for their services, what details they will need from you and your partner and by when, etc. This can sometimes just mean a 2-minute phone call. But start these conversations EARLY and this will help you plan your wedding better.

7. ALLOW TIME FOR RESEARCH.

As soon as someone says wedding, prices increase dramatically. If you have left something too late into the game, you may have no choice but to pay up. But if you allow enough time to do research, to shop around, to get a few quotes and think about things, then you will not be rushed and pressured into a costly decision.

8. ALLOW TIME FOR ERRORS.

The same goes here as for point no. 7. If you order things weeks or even months earlier than they need to be —if you can that is —then you will have plenty of time to fix any mistakes or errors. Issues are inevitably going to come up. We had issues with our invitations and our party favours, and while we left plenty of time to fix the invites, we didn't leave enough time to fix the party favours. This could've easily been avoided had we allowed enough time, but oh well. We had accepted that things might not go as planned and that is ok; people are understanding of the fact that things happen.

9. FIND PEOPLE YOU CAN TRUST TO HELP YOU ORGANISE YOUR WEDDING.

The pressure of organising a wedding can fortunately be eased by those in your close circle. If organising a wedding is just not your cup of tea, there are wedding planners who do this for a living. But if you want to be part of all the fun —and it really is fun —and just need a bit of help, find people who ARE good at organising, and have a chat with them. They can give you tips and may even help you stay organised (hopefully I have been able to do so with this chapter too!). What I do highly recommend, is that you find a few people that you can trust to designate jobs to, maybe even throughout your wedding planning period, but especially on the day of your wedding. This will make the whole planning process a true team effort and you will be able to enjoy your wedding a lot more.

10. VISIT YOUR LOCAL WEDDING SHOWS.

This is a great way to see as many wedding suppliers in one go as possible. Not only will you get to meet with people face-to-face and be able to ask questions and enquire on the spot, but you can make use of any special offers and deals going on the day. Don't feel pressured into anything though, but do make the most of what's on offer to you as a fiancé!

Summary of Questions in this Chapter

YOUR STORY BUILDING BLOCK #1: ORGANISATION SKILLS

What are your organising skills like?

If you were to rate your organisational skills on a scale from 1 to 10, with 1 being 'really poor' and 10 being 'organising queen', where would you be?

How do you feel about organising a wedding?

What is scaring you the most?

What are you most excited about?

Who could you speak to, to make the wedding planning process easier?

YOUR STORY BUILDING BLOCK #2: ORGANISATION TOOLS

How do you like to approach a project?

What means of learning do you prefer: visual, physical, aural, or any other style?

What tools do you want to set up to help you for your wedding planning?

What works well for you when it comes to organising?

What does NOT work well?

What have you done in the past that you have successfully organised?

What did you learn from that experience?

How do you want to sort all your wedding-related things?

How do you want to record and remind yourself of all your dates and deadlines?

What things will you need to buy?

What things will you need to prepare?

When can you set all your organising tools up? Set a date!

YOUR STORY BUILDING BLOCK #3: MAJOR MARKING POSTS

> *What big key items are on your list which make up the major marking posts towards your wedding?*
> *Who could you talk to, to find out if you've forgotten any major marking posts?*

YOUR STORY BUILDING BLOCK #4: GUIDING QUESTION FOR RANKING

> *What might your guiding question be to help you rank your major marking posts?*

YOUR STORY BUILDING BLOCK #5: THOUGHTFUL QUESTIONS FOR RANKING

> *How do you want to rank your marking posts?*
> *What are the most important?*
> *What are the most urgent?*
> *What might be something that you need to give particular focus to for your wedding?*
> *What items can you leave until closer to the wedding date?*

YOUR STORY BUILDING BLOCK #6: HELPFUL QUESTIONS

> *How do you want to make note of your marking posts and your wedding day goal?*
> *How will you decide on the date of the wedding day?*
> *What happens if your choice venue/supplier isn't available that date?*
> *What are your back up dates?*
> *Knowing your final date, what are the deadlines for*

your major marking posts?

Who can you talk to, to find out about dates and deadlines for each of your marking posts?

YOUR STORY BUILDING BLOCK #7: REFLECTION QUESTIONS

How do you feel about your overall wedding plan?

Who else, other than yourself, needs to know about these dates and deadlines?

YOUR STORY BUILDING BLOCK #8: WEDDING SHOWS

What public wedding events are accessible for you that you can attend?

Who could you speak to—staff at your wedding venue, your photographer, etc.—who might be able to recommend other wedding vendors and suppliers?

What wedding shows do the wedding vendors and suppliers display at?

YOUR STORY BUILDING BLOCK #9: WEDDING VENDORS AND SUPPLIERS

Which wedding vendors do you know you are definitely going to hire?

Which areas do you need to do some research in to find people?

Who could you talk to—friends, family, etc.—that can help you find people?

Who works in or near that particular industry (photography, makeup artistry, etc.) that might know someone who does weddings?

YOUR STORY BUILDING BLOCK #10: MARRIAGE CEREMONY AND CELEBRANT

What do you need to consider for your marriage ceremony and celebrant (different countries, different religions, different laws, etc.)?

How much time will you need to allow to work through the paperwork?

How many celebrants/ceremonies will you be having?

YOUR STORY BUILDING BLOCK #11: THE DAY OF PLANNING QUESTIONS

What could you prepare for your wedding day to make things go smoother?

Who can you give these items to, to take care of?

What items do you want to prepare for your wedding day?

Where or who with can you leave these items?

YOUR STORY BUILDING BLOCK #12: SPARES

What spare items will you need for:

The pre-ceremony preparation?

The ceremony?

Between ceremony and reception?

The reception?

The wedding photoshoot?

How will you confirm everyone's roles in the wedding day (before the day)?

How else can you reduce the responsibilities on you on your wedding day, and make your role easier?

YOUR STORY BUILDING BLOCK #13: DESIGNATED PEOPLE

What jobs need to be done throughout your wedding

day?

Who can you designate these jobs to?

If you are currently responsible for some of these jobs, how can you give this job to someone else?

Who do you trust the most?

Who do you definitely NOT trust doing these jobs? (Rule some people out!)

When can you speak to these people and organise these jobs (before the wedding day)?

Bonus Material

Wedding Planning Timeline

Here is a plain template of the wedding planning timeline I used. If you have small enough writing, feel free to write on this one; otherwise, you can head to www.letsgetyourlifetogether.com/bridalcoaching to download a free digital version.

The following instructions are a little recap on how to create your timeline:

1. Break down your wedding into the big main parts.

2. Look at these main parts and break these down into all the big items along the journey towards your end goal: your wedding day. Make this list 15 items or less to ensure a broad, simple plan. These 15 items or less will form your **major marking posts**.

3. Rank your items in order of priority. Choose a guiding question to help you rank (for example, we used urgency: which items need to be booked in first?).

4. Once you have your ranked list, draw them onto your timeline, as per page 48.

5. Once you have your wedding date, go back and start dating each of the major marking posts, for when they need to be completed by.

78

Wedding Day Survival Kit

Below is a list of all the potential items you could put in your Wedding Day Survival Kit. This list is to give you ideas, and is not exhaustive. You very well might think of other items that are not here.

- Painkillers
- Tissues
- Lipstick
- Deodorant
- Mini perfume
- Wet wipes (for wiping your underarms, sticky hands after eating and any dirt marks on your clothing)
- Chewing gum, mints or mouthwash
- Small snacks
- Water
- Band-Aids/plasters/bandages
- Blister bandages
- A small jacket if it's a cold day
- Sunscreen if it's a hot day
- Small compact umbrella
- Spare contact lenses/backup glasses
- Sunglasses
- Money
- I.D.
- Small hand mirror
- Toothpicks
- Any medication you need to take
- Any straps for existing injuries
- Spare socks
- Nail clippers for those annoying little skin bits on the edge of your nails that might irritate you (personally, these drive me nuts)

Further Reading on Practical Bits

- *Atomic Habits* by James Clear

This book has some helpful tips on creating habits, which can easily be applied to improving your organisation skills, including how to avoid procrastination.

- *The Power of Focus* by Jack Canfield, Mark Victor Hansen and Les Hewitt

This handy book is brimming with information, tips, quotes and exercises to help increase your focus on your goal, whatever that may be (in this case, your wedding).

Communication

A wedding has many moving parts, with many people coming together and working together. I never realised just how much of a collaboration a wedding is! All these people are going to work together through relationships, and therefore, they are going to need to communicate.

Communication makes up every single relationship we have with the people around us. Quite literally, a relationship only exists when you communicate with someone; with family and friends, with salespeople or service providers, with your local grocer. Communications are the exchange of information, i.e., a message you want to relay. They can be verbal or non-verbal, digital or behavioural, and can engage any of our senses. Some communications can be unique to particular people; how they word or punctuate a text. Even not saying anything communicates something.

As such, communication is part of everything in your wedding, and a successful wedding will depend on good communication. It relates to every single chapter in this book, so you will see it mentioned everywhere. But it is so important that it warrants a chapter on its own.

When communications fail, people become paranoid,

untrusting and suspicious. They can also feel excluded. A lack of communication can also cause wedding orders to be delivered at the wrong times, important key players to miss meetings, and inappropriate decisions. Overall, things will fall apart when there is a lack of communication.

In this chapter, I will show you how to customise your ways of communicating to best suit your situation for your wedding planning period. After all, for some people, this will be the most collaborative event you ever do with your family and friends!

Your Story Brain Dump Space

My Story

When it comes to communicating effectively, I like to consider some of the Bums on a Goal Post (see below). You've probably been taught some version of this when you were in primary school. For the Bums on a Goal Post version, each W (each 'bum') stands for Who, What, Where, When, and Why. The H shape (the 'goal post') stands for How. Sounds juvenile, but I bet you'll remember it!

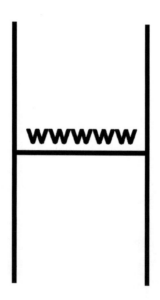

WHO

When it comes to communicating, the first W to consider is the WHO. Who will you need to be communicating with for your wedding?

An obvious answer would be your partner of course. Contrary to stereotypes, the wedding is not all about the bride; it's about the couple, and your partner will very much be part of your wedding planning. So, this is Person Number One you'll be communicating with.

Weddings are events for family and friends, and it is likely you will be closely communicating with parents, siblings, and best friends. Some of you might be in the situation where your parents are paying for your wedding, and that will require lots of communication.

You will also be communicating with all the wedding vendors and suppliers who will be contributing to your day—the reception venue staff, photographers, florists, etc.

And lastly of course, YOU will be communicating. Think about how you feel about that, because communicating this much might be new to you.

The WHO are basically all of your key players. The question of who you will need to communicate with might have an obvious answer for you, and that is great. For others, it might be more complicated. Maybe you have split families, family quarrels that are coming to the surface with your wedding, or other hurdles to overcome that will influence how you answer the WHO of your wedding communications.

Maybe you are in a similar situation as I was, where some of the people you need to communicate with are not in the same city or country as you are. The biggest part of our communication story was having Luke—the groom—in New Zealand. He was obviously a big part of the wedding, so needed to be included and told about all things wedding-related. Because our parents were paying for our wedding, we essentially had a little team to communicate amongst—Luke, myself, Luke's parents and my parents.

YOUR STORY BUILDING BLOCK #14.A: WHO YOU WILL BE COMMUNICATING WITH

Who will you need to communicate closely with for your wedding planning?

Where are they located in the world?

YOUR STORY BUILDING BLOCK #14.B: MORE ABOUT WHO YOU WILL BE COMMUNICATING WITH

What are they like when it comes to communicating?

How invested are they in the success of your wedding?

Who do you feel most comfortable communicating with?

Who are you dreading communicating with?

How can you make these communications easier?

What are your communication levels like?

What concerns do you have with your own communication levels?

What are you good at when it comes to communicating?

WHICH

An additional W word to those on the goal post could be WHICH. I swap Why out for WHICH, as WHICH is sometimes more useful. Once the WHO is established, then it is a matter of deciding WHICH platform you are going to use to communicate. This means considering which communication methods will suit the key players. There are SO MANY platforms through which you can communicate these days. Everyone has different preferences; you might already know of certain ways that are particularly effective for communicating with particular people. Here is a list of some communicating

methods:
1. Email
2. Group text
3. Phone calls
4. WhatsApp groups
5. Facebook message groups
6. Face-to-face meetings
7. Project management apps and tools such as Trello
8. Google calendar invites
9. Video chat calls through FaceTime, Skype, etc.
10. Notes around the house
11. Sign language
12. Different signs and symbols, emojis, etc.
13. Spreadsheets and tables

What other methods of communication can you think of?

Some of these will be better suited to different people, but some will also be better suited to different situations. For example, if you're in a different country to the person you need to communicate with, obviously in-person face-to-face meetings are not possible. For the duration of my time in New Zealand at the beginning of our engagement, and the rest of Luke's time in New Zealand (up until a month before the wedding), we communicated via email and free iPhone messages. Luckily there is not a huge time difference between New Zealand and Adelaide (only 2.5 hours), so we were also able to almost always have phone calls in real time.

When it comes to wedding vendors and suppliers, they will have their own preferred means of communicating too. A lot of the suppliers we engaged with sent us quotes and contacted us via email. This was very easy to forward emails onto our parents and Luke, so we utilised email a lot. Both of our dads used email regularly, and so I knew they would receive my emails in good time. So that Luke's mum was notified as well, I did have a group text message set up with myself and both of Luke's parents. Every time I sent an email through to my father-in-law, I would also send a text to the little group simply saying, "look out for an email from me—it has [this] in it", and sometimes also gave a quick summary of the main details. For my own mum, who didn't have email at the time, it was easier to keep her up to date because I lived with my parents during my time in Adelaide and would just verbally update her. Luke's parents, my parents, and I would also meet up quite regularly to discuss things face-to-face. I would say it was probably at least once a month. This was not like a scheduled meeting on the first Tuesday of every month or anything; sometimes it was just a genuine catch-up dinner and we would use the opportunity to discuss a few wedding details. Other times it was, say, a meeting with the DJ and all the parents would come, and then maybe we would go to one of our houses for a quick coffee and discuss anything from the meeting prior. At the time of our wedding, both our mums were working part-time jobs, so the 2 mums and myself would also catch-up regularly for coffees, wedding dress appointments, florist shopping, flower girl dress shopping, etc. As a result, we utilised many methods of communicating.

When it comes to deciding on which communication methods to use, the people you are communicating with need to be considered. If you are young and quite on top of digital communications, you might prefer to communicate on digital platforms, but this might not be the case for all the people you need to communicate with. Despite this, communicating face-to-face has a few advantages over the others. You can discuss an item and come up with a solution, all in one sitting. Communication is also not only about the words we use either; when we communicate, there is body language, inflections and intonations in our speech, and sounds like sighs and hesitations that all communicate something to us too (more on this later). In face-to-face conversations you get the full communication experience, engaging multiple human senses. But some people will feel uncomfortable communicating in-person, and might need that digital barrier for more successful communications, which is fine too. You will just need to consider people's preference. For example, I know not to email my mum anything because she doesn't check her email regularly. But my dad, and Luke's dad, are active on email for work and I know they will see my messages in their inbox and update themselves. Not all of our parents are on Facebook or WhatsApp, so I knew a group message on either of these platforms wouldn't be inclusive, but a group text message would be, as everyone has a mobile phone. Luke and I were active everywhere, so it was the parents I needed to consider more carefully.

While communicating with Luke and our parents dominated, there were also other parties we needed to communicate with, such as the bridal party. Your bridal party is usually younger than your parents and similar in age to you. My bridesmaids were all under 25 years old at the time, so a Facebook group message made better sense as a method of communication. They also communicated through another Facebook group that did not include me, the bride, and as far as I am aware, they also had a couple of their own meetings face-to-face. The groomsmen had a similar Facebook group message going on as well, with and without Luke. Communicating with the suppliers was another preference yet again. After the initial face-to-face meetings, most of them preferred emails and phone calls. Only my make-up artist used text messaging in addition to phone calls. But everyone had their own style.

All of this might sound excessively detailed to you, but this is only because I have written it all out in one lump. If you pause and think about it, you are probably already unconsciously aware of the preferred methods of communication of those closest to you, and this might only require a few seconds of thought to become *consciously* aware of it. This is how you increase your self-awareness, by consciously choosing to stop, think, and become aware of the fact that you already know this. It is important to know the answers to these questions, as if you don't get the platform right, people might miss important messages. And if you don't know someone's preferred method of communication, you can always ask them to get your expectations aligned.

YOUR STORY BUILDING BLOCK #15: WHICH METHODS OF COMMUNICATION

What methods of communication do you prefer?

What methods of communication do the other key players prefer?

What methods of communication do you know definitely DO NOT work for you/others?

What communication disabilities might you have to work with?

Who else could you discuss these questions with?

HOW MUCH

The next letter from the goal post to consider is the goal post itself—the HOW. But this is a different kind of how that needs to be considered, and that is HOW MUCH to communicate. In the Money chapter, I talk about how people can be immediately more on guard when it comes to spending their money, and how they're usually more likely to spend when you are more transparent with how it is being spent. Being transparent comes down to good communication.

Let's break down 'transparency'. I will give you a childhood example to demonstrate this.

As a kid, whenever I asked my parents for some money, my parents would always reply with, "What for?". Even if I just wanted a couple of dollars for an ice-cream at the school canteen, they still wanted to know what the money was for. The second I resisted answering that question, I created suspicion in my parents' mind and my chances of getting my ice-cream decreased. After a while, I knew to expect this question, so instead of waiting for them to ask it of me, I stayed one step ahead. I pre-empted that question and explained the reason with the request, every time, i.e., "It's really hot today and I'd really like an ice-cream. Could I please have some money for an ice-cream today?". I was transparent with my spending of their money. The second I tried to hide what I was spending it on, the less likely I was to receive the money. I learnt that when I explained the reason behind my request, then they understood my request. UNDERSTANDING is a big part of being transparent.

The second part of being transparent is being clear in your explanations. If I went to my parents and asked, "Can I please have some money for a toy? Oh, can I have a cup of hot chips?! No wait! Look there's a sale on this book, I'm going to get that too! Can I please?", then they are probably just as confused as I am about what I am going to spend their money on. Until I made up my mind and explained just one thing I was going to buy, then I would not receive any money. I had to be CLEAR in explaining my intentions with the money. This also contributed to being transparent.

Let's now scale that up to the wedding Luke and I had. When it comes down to a 20-something like me telling our four 50-something parents how to spend their money, the lessons I learnt as a kid still applied. Our parents wanted to be reassured that their money was going to good use, and whenever I asked them to make a payment, the clearer I was with my explanation, the better. At the end of the day, I am still their child, so there can still be that parent-child dynamic going on. Sometimes, even in our early 20s, some parents still do not see their child as an adult. This time could still be a transition period for both the parents and the young adult. For me, I was 23 years old when we were planning our wedding, and I knew I wanted to step up as an adult and handle our wedding planning maturely.

I personally have always come across as 'mature' for my age with regards to such tasks; my parents know me well and trusted me with the wedding preparations. But this wasn't necessarily the case for my in-laws. Generally, your in-laws don't know you as well as your own parents do, and so it is important to gain their trust, especially if you are handling their money as I was. With Luke in New Zealand, I had no choice but to communicate directly with his parents. Prior to this, I think it is fair to say I probably used to speak to them through Luke a lot more. 'Old me' would have found it a lot easier to have Luke ask his parents to make a wedding payment, instead of me asking my soon-to-be in-laws. But without Luke directly involved on the ground, I had no choice but to do it myself. I figured what worked well for my parents *might* work well for Luke's parents, so I applied my little transparency lesson from my childhood to my communications with them too, and sure enough that worked really well. The huge benefit of this was that it deepened my relationship with my now parent-in-laws. During that time, they were able to see how I handled everything, and they increased their trust in me as a life partner for their son. I tell you what though, when it came to the wedding, I was asking for a lot more than a couple of dollars for an ice-cream! I definitely found it uncomfortable at first asking my parents, and even more so my in-laws, to make payments. Asking parents for anything *can* be a bit of a power-struggle for some. Fortunately, after my first couple of super polite requests, both sets of our parents were incredibly obliging, and we continued in this respectful, reasonable and cooperative manner throughout the wedding planning.

Being transparent doesn't lend itself only to successful requests. Communication is the exchange of information. Being transparent applies whether you are requesting something or are on the receiving end too, i.e., you can be transparent with your replies. For example, say your mum asks you, "What would you like for your wedding dress?" She is requesting information from you, and you can be transparent with your answer by *clearly* explaining what you would like for your wedding dress, with reasons behind your choices. "How do you explain clearly?" I hear you ask. I use this Rule of Thumb: **Explain in a way that if you had to explain it to a 5-year-old, they would understand.** This is not to say *treat* who you are speaking to as a 5-year-old. This means, use simple words, don't use any jargon, be concise (no verbal vomit), speak at an easy pace that is not too fast, and use a structure that flows easily. To your mum's question, you could reply with the following, "Because cream suits my skin colour, I would like a cream-coloured dress". Everyone can understand the words in this sentence. It was clear, there was no confusion, and the words that construct this sentence are simple, easy words. A complicated version of this reply could be, "Because cool white doesn't suit my warm-toned olive skin, I would like a warm-toned off-white dress." Unless you are familiar with cool and warm tones with respect to colours, then you won't necessarily understand this sentence, and this causes misunderstandings when communicating with people. That reply also states 3 different colours—cool white, warm-toned olive, and warm-toned off-white—which can get muddled up in people's heads and again, cause confusion or miscommunications.

You may have noticed that, in my replies above, both for the 'ice-cream as a kid' example and the 'reply to my mum's wedding dress question' example, I put the reason first:

Reason: "It's really hot today and I'd really like an ice-cream…

Request: "…Could I please have some money for an ice-cream today?"

Reason: "Because white doesn't suit my skin colour…

Request: "…I would like a cream-coloured dress."

This was intentional. When you communicate with someone, they will hear the above examples in the order of how they are written or said. When you put the *reason* first, the *understanding* also comes first. People are more open to the request when they already understand where it is coming from. When we state the request first, an alarm bell can automatically go off in the brain of the person on the receiving end, which screams, "WHY?" They don't understand the request, and unconsciously they will block it. The reason which follows then has to work twice as hard, first to break down that block, and *then* to increase understanding.

You can practice this in conversations with your family and friends and see what happens. Listen out for it in other people's communications to you as well. Listening and becoming aware of little details like this will increase your awareness and help you make any changes that you'd like to make to your communication skills.

To summarise, being transparent involves 2 key points:

1. Help the other person UNDERSTAND
2. Explain it CLEARLY

This way of being transparent also promotes INCLUSION. For communications with Luke's and my parents, by explaining what a payment was for, by explaining details they asked me about, I was including our parents in the decision-making, and that is always a nice feeling, especially for a wedding. Lack of inclusion can cause feelings like frustration and anxiety to the people who want or need to be involved. Luke's parents could have wondered, "Why hasn't Juliet told me what that money was for?!" and this breaks down trust. This does not make them feel secure that I am managing their money, or the wedding, appropriately. The same might apply for you with your parents, or your partner, or any other key players in your wedding. Being transparent will promote inclusion, and thus, trust.

You will notice that I have been using the words 'asking' and 'requesting' instead of 'telling' throughout these examples too. Asking someone something, even if they have no choice but to go ahead, will deepen that feeling of inclusion as well. It will also give them some responsibility and a sense of choice in the decision. The *sense* or *feeling* of choice is what matters. Everyone likes this feeling because it empowers us. When we *tell* someone to do something, it can come across as dictatorial, maybe even patronising, and we automatically feel negative about doing the task. It takes away that empowerment. Sometimes we even put up some resistance and do not feel like doing the task at all simply because we were *told* to do it. Think about it: "Pay this bill please" has a totally different impact to, "Can you please pay this bill?" If my parents were on the receiving end, they would be experiencing a completely different feeling if I asked them the *question* version rather than the *demand* version. *Asking* my parents if they could make a payment instead of *telling* them to make a payment is also more respectable. I am respecting their involvement in the decision, and not just because they are my parents; everyone likes to feel respected, especially in a team environment.

Being transparent is going to help communications with all the key players in your wedding—suppliers, vendors, etc. But, while being more transparent will help your communications in some areas, also have a little judgement when it comes to HOW MUCH you need to communicate with people outside the key players. This is the opposite end of HOW MUCH you need to communicate. You may be happy to share all with everyone—a wedding is a wedding, most details will be revealed in due time so you might not see the point in any secrecy (unless there is a surprise for the day of course). But knowing the real detail in your wedding is usually on a need-to-know basis. So, extended family members or friends who ask you about these kinds of details—finances, wedding dress details, etc.—don't really need to know this information, especially if you don't want them to. There are also those rare people out there who tend to dig for information, like aunty so-and-so who is just having a nosy and wants to have her 2 cents' worth. Wedding details are typically none of these people's business in the lead up to a wedding. They have no influence in the wedding, therefore if you don't want to communicate details with them, pay them no mind. But avoiding these communications is the tricky part. So firstly, simply decide how much (or rather, how little) wedding detail you wish to share with people beyond your key players. Secondly—and this is my TIP for avoiding the conversations—when you're in a conversation with someone who is probing too far for your liking, I found simply making it a humorous game made them go away: "You will have to wait and see!". Sticking to this response stubbornly made the probers laugh and go away. Rarely do people argue with this response, because there's really nothing to argue in it. Humour is a very clever tool for tricky situations. It will give you your desired outcome, whilst keeping the air light and avoiding creating tension.

YOUR STORY BUILDING BLOCK #16: HOW MUCH YOU WILL BE COMMUNICATING

How transparent are you in your current communications?

How comfortable are you with asking for things from certain people?

Following your answer from the question above, what is it that makes you feel like that when asking for something?

How could you improve your transparency when communicating with key players?

How transparent do you NEED to be in your communications with different people?

What will be the consequences of this choice?

What communication strategies do you want to use?

HOW

Let's summarise so far. I have spoken about deciding on the WHO you need to be communicating with, WHICH methods of communication you're going to use, and HOW MUCH you are going to communicate with different parties. Now we will look at the common HOW: how to communicate effectively.

Let's start with how to communicate on disagreements, because, take it from me, they *just might* pop up when planning your wedding. When you are communicating with lots of people, everyone will have a different opinion. With any group of people, not everyone will agree. AND THAT IS OK. It's ok to disagree. This is a fact of life that has somewhat fallen through the gaps between all the boxes the world tries to put us in, and needs to be accepted again. In order to move forward on disagreements, those involved need to agree to disagree. This is the ultimate agreement. So, it's how you handle a disagreement that will either help or hinder your relationships.

For example, my father-in-law and I disagreed on who should walk me down the aisle. He believed in the traditional way that the bride's father walks his daughter down the aisle. I was of the opinion that the tradition stems from the days when a daughter used to be the property of her father, and was being 'given away' to become the property of her soon-to-be husband. I didn't agree with this because I am no one's property, so I didn't want this tradition. But my father-in-law had never even thought of it like that; he only saw a beautiful father-daughter tradition that had been one in his family for many years. I respected his opinion and I felt he respected mine. The fact was that we were able to discuss this in a conversation, and while we could see where the other was coming from, we weren't changing our own opinions, so in the end we agreed to disagree. That is a great resolution to a disagreement. His opinion did not hugely affect this detail in our wedding anyway; it only affected my father and I. As a result, we were each able to discuss this topic with a level-head and did not let our emotions get involved. In fact, it was my father-in-law who really instilled in me the resolution to 'agree to disagree'. Everyone involved in our wedding didn't have to agree with everything in our wedding; they just had to accept it.

Sometimes agreeing to disagree is not an option, particularly if a decision needs to be made. If a conversation does become heated and tensions arise, leaving that topic for a few days or weeks and putting a little extra private thought into the issue almost always helps. Emotions can cool down, and rational thinking can come back into play. Some things don't even end up being worth arguing over. But when emotions are high, we say things we don't mean, shouting can happen, feelings can get hurt, and trust can be broken. It can be really detrimental to a relationship if emotions get too high and aren't kept in check, and communication levels can completely break down. When you move into this high-emotion space, you can become even firmer on your own opinion, and it is harder to resolve an issue when you're in that space. So, it is always a good idea to pause the conversation, cool down, go away and think a bit more in your own space, and then return to the issue another day. This more often than not is enough to resolve a problem.

Failing that, you can consider the WHICH question of communication again, in the context of the disagreement; which platform would this disagreement better suit? For example, I know I tend to raise the volume of my voice when I'm in an angry or frustrated high-emotion state and Luke doesn't like this, so that has generally made our disagreements worse. In these situations we pause the disagreement, take a step back, cool for a bit, and change the platform of our disagreement to texting. We almost always come to a resolution when we do this. The digital platform has removed all volume, and that extra layer of translating feelings and thoughts into words actually makes for better communication and understanding. You might find a platform change helps your disagreements too.

To summarise so far, we've discussed 3 options you could choose for disagreements:

---

1. Agree to disagree
2. Pause the conversation, cool down and come back to it another day
3. Change the platform you're communicating on

YOUR STORY BUILDING BLOCK #17: HOW YOU WILL COMMUNICATE ON DISAGREEMENTS

How do you like to resolve a disagreement?

What does NOT work well for you when resolving a disagreement?

What do you know works well in a disagreement, but is something you find hard to actually follow?

How does each of the key players like to resolve disagreements?

What makes things worse in a disagreement with each of your key players?

How can you come up with a way together to resolve wedding disagreements?

When can you organise to talk to your key players about disagreements?

What's going to break your trust in them and their trust

in you?
Who are you most concerned about disagreeing with?
How can you approach these particular people?
What can you do to improve these relationships?
What new strategies or methods do you want to try for any wedding disagreements that you have?

Earlier I mentioned a couple of benefits of communicating in-person and face-to-face; you can see the other person's body language, register any sighs or hesitations, etc. These play a big part in our communications. Albert Mehrabian's rule of communication states that, when having face-to-face conversations, our communication is broken down into the following:

1. **55% body language**
2. **38% tone of voice**
3. **7% spoken words**

These percentages represent the elements of communication that have the highest impact. The words we say actually don't count for much! It's *how* we say something that counts for the biggest impact—our tone of voice and our body language. So, when we communicate face-to-face or (to a lesser degree) on the phone with our partner, our parents, the bridal party, siblings, suppliers… ANYONE during this wedding planning period, we need to give attention to our body language and tone of voice.

This is particularly important for when it comes to communicating with parents. Here we can very easily slip into that parent-child relationship, especially in a disagreement, and our body language and tone of voice can really start to show that. We all have traits from our childhood as to how we communicate with our parents, and in high-emotion situations like a disagreement, it is easy to resort to these tendencies. Attitude, a sense to rebel, eye rolls and 'I don't care' vibes can come out of us, while our parents turn up the 'Parent' in them and start *telling* you what to do, and we already know what telling someone to do will result in. For some, especially those who are getting married relatively young, this might be an opportunity for you to show your parents the adult you are growing into. For others, maybe you are happy staying in that child space and letting your parents take the reins for your wedding. Regardless of your preferred set up, for a real collaborative experience it will be important to stay in an adult-to-adult discussion with your parents. This may involve asking your parents the hard question to let you be an adult in this process; not all parents are happy going from parent-child to adult-adult with their children. This is a life step which goes beyond just your wedding, but your wedding might be caught up in it. This step is a process, and by definition a process needs to involve time. As such, you'll need to respect time in the process and adopt a level of patience. This may continue past your wedding, but let's leave that for another book. During your wedding planning, you may need to remind and ask your parents repeatedly (this is where the patience comes in) that you're an adult here too now, and over time as your parents warm to this and see that yes that is correct and there's nothing they can do about that, acceptance can come.

When we communicate over email, through texts, even when we share spreadsheets and other files with others, we don't have the body language and tone of voice elements of communication, and yet we are still trying to communicate. Our communications are reduced to just text. Being able to explain your message clearly, in writing, so that the person on the receiving end understands it in the way that you intend, is a skill in itself. I'm certain that we have all experienced receiving a digital message and mistaken the meaning behind it, or realised that someone we sent a message to has misunderstood our message. Welcome to digital communications.

With Luke being overseas, and sending a number of quotes, proofs and options via text and email between him and also the parents, communications reduced to text-only was an important skill I had to develop. In order to do this, I followed a few guidelines in my messages, some that I have already mentioned earlier.

Guidelines for Written Communications

1. Help the other person understand.
2. Explain it clearly.
3. Ensure the intended message would be clear if a 5-year-old was reading it (Rule of Thumb for all communications).
4. Use simple, easy words (no jargon or big words).
5. Get to the point, without dragging it on.
6. Highlight main points in CAPITALS, bold or highlighter.
7. Ask for confirmation that they received a message, or alternatively ask a question in the message to encourage a response.
8. Offer the receiver to 'ask any questions' if they need further clarification.

I find point number 3, the Rule of Thumb, super useful for

communicating over digital platforms. Something that I'm reminded of here is reading in Ashlee Vance's book *Elon Musk: How the Billionaire CEO of SpaceX and Tesla is Shaping our Future* that Elon Musk asked his team to not use acronyms in email communications. These days we try and communicate as fast as possible and there's a multitude of acronyms out there that have been developed to help that. We assume others know their meanings but, truth is, sometimes they don't, but don't want to admit it. They go along pretending they knew what we meant. This leads to miscommunications. This is just one example, but be conscious of this if you're an acronym user, and be sure to clarify the person on the receiving end is understanding your message well. Most 5-year-olds don't use acronyms, so sticking to this Rule of Thumb may just cover that anyway.

WHO I'm communicating with will also influence my style of message. For example, if I were to communicate with a wedding supplier or someone I was working with in a professional capacity, my messages would be polite and professional, with a formal greeting and sign off. Whereas, with my dad and my father-in-law, I know they are men of few words and don't like a lot of 'fluff' words (words that are there to form a proper sentence but aren't 100% needed to get the message across). I know they prefer straight-to-the-point messages, so if I only needed a few words to convey my message, then that was fine. If I did that to my mum though, she'd think I was being short with her and was upset with her.

Different people can have different little quirks too. For example, with Luke, from when we started dating and until this day, I know he doesn't like to use full stops in his text messages. To him, full stops in a text message appear blunt and angry, so he will only use them when he is angry at me. Recent polls have shown that apparently, he's not the only one. I have also adopted this quirk when messaging him, so if we are happy, our sentences will end in commas, and if we are not happy with each other. We. Use. Full. Stops.

YOUR STORY BUILDING BLOCK #18: HOW YOU COMMUNICATE ON DIGITAL PLATFORMS

What are you like when you are communicating via digital platforms?

How often do you experience misunderstandings because of misinterpreted text-only messages?

What can you deduce from that answer?

What guidelines would you like to follow to ensure clear communications on digital platforms?

Who else do you need to discuss this with?

Wedding communications: make or break relationships?

In our families, it's tradition for our parents to pay for our wedding, so they were communicated with regularly and were very much involved with the wedding planning process. This could have gone either of 2 ways: really well, or really bad. Fortunately for us it went really well; our wedding truly was a huge family bonding experience. A large part of this was due to the level of communication. It was also due to a genuine interest in our wedding. When you are genuinely interested in something, you are engaged and are willing to be cooperative. Between the 6 of us—Luke and myself, my 2 parents and Luke's 2 parents— the key factor was that we were all invested in the same goal: creating our happy wedding. When you are invested in something, you will put in the extra effort to make it work, and will willingly contribute to a smooth operation. If putting in the extra effort to make it work means communicating better, then that's what you're happy to do. Our families got along famously and everyone wanted us to be married (seems humorous to say this but some families do not want their kids to marry—I have known of a couple of these!). We all cooperated constructively and made the effort to communicate well.

Because that is exactly what it takes to communicate: effort. Communication is quite literally the key to the door of good relationships. The better you communicate, the better the relationship. With good communication, all parties in the relationship feel more secure in the relationship. The more I opened up and practised my own communication skills, the more those around me responded positively to it, and my relationships with Luke and our family have improved. During our wedding period we had some of the best levels of communication ever between the 6 of us, and since our wedding our communication has stayed up there. So overall, the team effort resulted in more than just a successful wedding; it deepened our relationships.

This will not necessarily be your experience with everyone, and it's unfortunate when it's with your own family members or friends. Sometimes you and so-and-so get along famously, but are just not compatible when it comes to working on projects together, and planning a wedding with people so involved can sometimes break a relationship. Incompatibility is not necessarily a bad thing; just because you are clashing and can't plan a wedding with so-and-so, doesn't mean they aren't a good friend or cousin or sibling or whoever. Keep in mind that this wedding time will pass, and it's the relationship that will remain, in whatever state it comes out as. Time does heal wounds, but if you are responsible for any amends that need to be made, do so. You will feel better when you have done your part. That is the only part you can control: YOU. YOU can also forgive the person, because forgiveness is about you, not about the other person. It doesn't mean to pretend nothing ever happened and dismiss any hurt; there will always be a lesson to be learnt in a major quarrel. But you can forgive.

Forgiveness is a tricky one to get the hang of. Personally, I find it can depend on my present emotional state. If I'm in a good mood, I'm more likely to feel forgiving, and the reverse is also true. The way I have approached forgiveness is by being understanding. This seems to help me, and hey if it has a chance at helping you to forgive too then I am happy to pass it on.

I try to see the WHY behind someone's actions that I felt hurt by. I paint a little story in my head of any facts I know: they're tired, they've had to deal with difficult people all day, their parents have a similar trait and they've always copied it, it's not their fault, they're feeling a bit jealous, they're on the defensive, they feel attacked, etc. It's all hypothetical and I have no idea of knowing if any of it is true, or what is the actual truth. The real truth is, when someone does something that you feel hurt by, more often than not it's more about them than you. It also *tells* you more about them than you. There's a reason they have acted or reacted that way, and it's not necessarily your position to know why, but you can still be understanding that, yes, there is a reason why they've behaved that way, and it's often got nothing to do with you. It may not hurt any less, but empathising with them can help the forgiveness process. If I get the chance to sit with that person and we can talk it out so both of us can understand (more communicating!), then maybe we can share apologies, or maybe not. This doesn't always happen, and so it needs to be let go of and forgiven. This is for you. Not them, YOU. What you can take from the experience is this: as I said, whatever went down tells you something about THEM. This is a lesson. It might be a lesson on how to approach this person in future, or that the two of you don't really match at all, and the relationship slowly ends up discontinuing. Whatever it is, there's a lesson here somewhere, so think about this and discover that lesson.

Don't let yourself off the hook here too easy though; do take this opportunity to check in with your own behaviour. If you yourself were unreasonably hurtful in the first place and that provoked the other person's reactions, own up and make amends. Think about the WHY behind your own behaviour and learn something about yourself here. For example, maybe it's best to avoid that kind of conversation when you're tired because you have less patience in that tired state. If you simply had to make a hard decision and break the news to someone, soften it as much as you can, but still extend understanding to the other person's reaction if it did hurt. You definitely may not have provoked the other person's behaviour at all, but may be able to better define what you do and don't like in relationships, now that you've discovered something that you find hurtful. Do check in and reflect on your own behaviour, because the lesson to be learnt may indeed be about yourself. You don't want to miss that.

Also note that communications can make or break a relationship with wedding professionals too. For us, one particular person fell off the face of the earth, and I really struggled to get hold of them. If you cannot get hold of someone, then you cannot communicate, and this did not bode well for the relationship. This person was very frustrating to work with, and I did not trust this person as a result. These kinds of poor services pop up every now and then. You can dump them or deal with them. We chose the latter because it was too late in the game to change. Fortunately, they performed fine on the wedding day, but after everything was said and done, I will not be recommending them. Ah, the age of reviews.

YOUR STORY BUILDING BLOCK #19: RELATIONSHIPS MAKE OR BREAK

How close are you to the people you need to communicate with?
How important is the relationship to you?
What might be the consequences to any broken relationships post-wedding?
How can you help to 'make' the relationships and strengthen them for post-wedding times?

Communication Tools

You are not always going to be around to do all the communicating when it comes to your wedding planning, but, if it's your style, there are tools you can create to do the communicating for you. For example, a really neat and clear spreadsheet will successfully communicate all your wedding expenditures, and a great spreadsheet will communicate to you in just a quick glance whether you have stuck to your budget or not (money stuff coming up!). I found it particularly useful to set up a few tools for the actual day of the wedding, because I knew, being the bride, I'd be rather pre-occupied, and I'd rather tools do the communicating work for me. These were introduced in Practical Bits as organisational tools as well. Return to that chapter for more detail, but to briefly summarise:

- I created a schedule for the morning of the wedding. This

schedule communicated where everyone needed to be and at what time. This was particularly detailed so I did a separate schedule just for the morning.

- I created a schedule for the entire day. This was an itinerary that communicated all the deliveries, all the times for the photographers, videographers and limousine drivers, and the times for the food and proceedings at the reception.

- I set up a table of contact numbers for the photographer, the videographer, the DJ, the florist, the cake maker, and the venue wedding coordinator, so that they could communicate between them.

The point of these communication tools was to take Luke and I out of the equation. A great communication tool will do this for you. As you can see from the list above, your communication tools for your wedding are likely to be in a written format, so keep to the guidelines for written communications discussed earlier, or create your own guidelines.

The DESIGN of your communication tools will also have an impact. You don't want this complicated colour-coded map that people need instructions on how to read; you want the design to be just as simple and clear as the information it is displaying. For schedules, spreadsheets and contacts list, text in a simple table usually does the job very well. Most wedding related information is usually in the form of lists and numbers, and a table is an appropriate way to communicate that. I used a few colours to *help*, not *hinder*, the communications. For example, for my morning schedule, each person had their own colour, so if someone wanted to know where they were supposed to be, all they needed to do was find all the red, say. Looking for a colour on a sheet of paper is quicker than reading through information. Keep the design of your communication tools in mind when you are planning them out. You don't need to go do a graphic design course or anything; just spend a couple of minutes of thought on how to make your communication tools really easy to read. Overall, a good communication tool is a small thing to set up, but has a big pay-off.

YOUR STORY BUILDING BLOCK #20: COMMUNICATION TOOLS

How much do you want to be communicated with on the wedding day?

How can you remove yourself from the equation for communications between the photographer, caterer, florist, etc.?

What communication tools could help you?

What format will suit each of your communication tools? When can you create these?

Suggestion Box

1. DECIDE HOW YOU ARE GOING TO COMMUNICATE.

How we communicate is so important. This includes the method of communication and the quantity of communication. If this is an area that you are concerned about and can potentially foresee issues arising, I highly recommend sitting with the people you need to communicate with early on in the wedding planning process, and really discuss the HOW of your communications. Getting your expectations all on the same page from the beginning will give you something to refer back to if people start changing things.

2. USE THE BEST METHODS OF COMMUNICATION AVAILABLE TO YOU.

In the age of digital communication, there are so many ways of communicating. Who you need to communicate with and what they are used to will usually determine which method of communication is going to be most appropriate. You want to use one that is going to work for everyone, as well as be the most effective method to work with. For example, there is no point messaging and sharing photos on a Facebook group if some of your key players don't use it, when you could be using a WhatsApp group which would work better if everyone does have a mobile phone.

3. DECIDE HOW YOU WILL RESOLVE DISAGREEMENTS.

This is another collaborative discussion, but one you can initiate. With such a big event as a wedding, there can be lots of people and lots of opinions. For the people that matter most, sit down and decide how you are going to resolve any disagreements, particularly when it involves a decision that needs to be made. Plan a strategy that suits your family, like the ones described in this chapter. Remember, not everyone needs to agree with everything in your wedding, so it is ok to resolve a disagreement by agreeing to disagree.

4. KEEP EVERYONE WHO NEEDS TO KNOW IN THE LOOP.

If there are people who need to know some information, then share it. I'm talking key players. The more information about the wedding they know, the more they will feel included and reassured. If you keep them in the loop, they are less likely to keep asking you for details and potentially verge on annoying you. They are also less likely to feel feelings of anxiety and frustration, because they will feel they can trust you're keeping them up to date. Overall, they'll be in better moods when they deal with you and will chase you less, and this will benefit you in the long run.

5. KEEP COMMUNICATIONS CLEAR AND SIMPLE.

When it comes to written communications —in actual fact, you can apply this to any form of communication — follow the Rule of Thumb: will a 5-year-old be able to understand this message? If the answer is yes, great job. If not, think how you can make the message as simple and as clear as possible. This will decrease the chances of any miscommunications or misunderstandings.

6. LET EVERYONE BE HEARD.

Almost by definition, we all think our own opinion is the most correct, and everyone likes to be heard. Let everyone have their opportunity to share. When we feel heard, and feel that our opinion has been considered, we are more likely to be cooperative, and even negotiate with greater flexibility. This is also conducive to an adult-to-adult conversation, and may very well raise points you had not considered, or cause you to change your opinion for something better.

7. GET PEOPLE TO CONFIRM THEY HAVE RECEIVED A MESSAGE.

When you send emails or texts, you can explicitly ask for a confirmation that they have read the message. Maybe you already have a 'read' function set up in your email or phone, or the receiver has that set up on their phone. If you aren't comfortable with asking for a confirmation, you can subtly ask a question in your message, which encourages the receiver to reply to you, and then that can essentially be used as your confirmation. You can also check on phone calls or in face-to-face meetings if they have received a message. This is particularly important when you organise a group meeting with lots of people. This confirmation is, in a way, a form of RSVP, so you can know who will be attending or if you need to organise an alternative time.

8. KEEP RECORDS OF COMMUNICATIONS.

Even in our face-to-face meetings, we wrote notes, shared photos, and sent each other quotes and numbers. We would also send a summary of our notes to the people in attendance so that everyone was in agreeance with what went down. There are a lot of details when it comes to wedding planning, so recording them will help you not forget them. This will also help when you need to refer back to something so-and-so supplier offered at that meeting months ago. It is a form of 'insurance' as I like to call it —prices that suppliers had previously agreed on can't be increased at a later date, because you recorded it in a previous meeting. So, record EVERYTHING.

9. TOUCH BASE REGULARLY WITH YOUR KEY PLAYERS.

This relates to point 4. By touching base regularly, you can update all the information people have. When it comes to the suppliers, you won't necessarily need to be in constant contact with them. Because of this, sometimes they can fall off the radar —this was the case for one of our suppliers. By touching base regularly, you can catch wind of any rogue suppliers early, and give yourself enough time to replace them if need be. You can keep them up to date with any details they need as well.

10. CREATE SOME COMMUNICATION TOOLS.

The point here is to take yourself out of the equation. What can you create that can communicate for you, without you? This could be a schedule or a table like I used, or it could be any other communication tool. Signs are a common method of communicating quickly. They say that a picture speaks a thousand words, so maybe you have drawn a bunch of visual signals to communicate a message. It could be anything! As long as the pay-off will be worth the time it takes to create a communication tool, then go for it. There may even be some out there already which could save you some time creating them yourself — take some templates from the internet (check out those provided in the Bonus Material sections of some of these chapters), or even some kind of app that sends reminders to a whole group.

Summary of Questions in this Chapter

YOUR STORY BUILDING BLOCK #14.A: WHO YOU WILL BE COMMUNICATING WITH

Who will you need to communicate closely with for your wedding planning?

Where are they located in the world?

YOUR STORY BUILDING BLOCK #14.B: MORE ABOUT WHO YOU WILL BE COMMUNICATING WITH

What are they like when it comes to communicating?

How invested are they in the success of your wedding?

Who do you feel most comfortable communicating with?

Who are you dreading communicating with?

How can you make these communications easier?

What are your communication levels like?

What concerns do you have with your own communication levels?

What are you good at when it comes to communicating?

YOUR STORY BUILDING BLOCK #15: WHICH METHODS OF COMMUNICATION

What methods of communication do you prefer?

What methods of communication do the other key players prefer?

What methods of communication do you know definitely DO NOT work for you/others?

What communication disabilities might you have to work with?

Who else could you discuss these questions with?

YOUR STORY BUILDING BLOCK #16: HOW MUCH YOU WILL BE COMMUNICATING

How transparent are you in your current communications?

How comfortable are you with asking for things from certain people?

Following your answer from the question above, what is it that makes you feel like that when asking for something?

How could you improve your transparency when communicating with key players?

How transparent do you NEED to be in your communications with different people?

What will be the consequences of this choice?

What communication strategies do you want to use?

YOUR STORY BUILDING BLOCK #17: HOW YOU WILL COMMUNICATE ON DISAGREEMENTS

How do you like to resolve a disagreement?

What does NOT work well for you when resolving a disagreement?

What do you know works well in a disagreement, but is something you find hard to actually follow?

How does each of the key players like to resolve disagreements?

What makes things worse in a disagreement with each of your key players?

How can you come up with a way together to resolve wedding disagreements?

When can you organise to talk to your key players about disagreements?

What's going to break your trust in them and their trust

in you?

Who are you most concerned about disagreeing with?

How can you approach these particular people?

What can you do to improve these relationships?

What new strategies or methods do you want to try for any wedding disagreements that you have?

YOUR STORY BUILDING BLOCK #18: HOW YOU COMMUNICATE ON DIGITAL PLATFORMS

What are you like when you are communicating via digital platforms?

How often do you experience misunderstandings because of misinterpreted text-only messages?

What can you deduce from that answer?

What guidelines would you like to follow to ensure clear communications on digital platforms?

Who else do you need to discuss this with?

YOUR STORY BUILDING BLOCK #19: RELATIONSHIPS MAKE OR BREAK

How close are you to the people you need to communicate with?

How important is the relationship to you?

What might be the consequences to any broken relationships post-wedding?

How can you help to 'make' the relationships and strengthen them for post-wedding times?

YOUR STORY BUILDING BLOCK #20: COMMUNICATION TOOLS

How much do you want to be communicated with on the wedding day?

How can you remove yourself from the equation for communications between the photographer, caterer, florist, etc.?

What communication tools could help you?

What format will suit each of your communication tools?

When can you create these?

Bonus Material

Communication Tool —Contacts List template

Over the page is the template that I used for making a contacts list. This list I distributed to all the key players so that if they needed to communicate between them, they didn't need to use me as a middleperson.

Head to www.letsgetyourlifetogether.com/bridalcoaching to download a digital copy of this template, which you can customise to suit your own wedding. Here you will also find digital versions of other communication tool templates covered in the Bonus Material sections of other chapters.

PHOTOGRAPHER	Name: Number: Email: Website: Address:
VIDEOGRAPHER	Name: Number: Email: Website: Address:
DJ / MC	Name: Number: Email: Website: Address:
CAKE MAKER	Name: Number: Email: Website: Address:
FLORIST	Name: Number: Email: Website: Address:

Further Reading on Communication

There is an endless supply of material out there on improving your communications, but here are a few on my bookshelf:

- *How to Deal with Difficult People* by **Gill Hasson**
I highly recommend this book, for communications in general and for family politics later on as well. It is a great book that gets to the point and is a fast and easy read. It helps to understand and, as the title suggests, deal with people you find difficult to work with.

- *The Communication Book* by **Mikael Krogerus and Roman Tschäppeler**
This is a handy little book with 44 easy little areas to improve your communication. Comes with doodles and all, because doodles can sometimes communicate better than text!

- *The Rules of People* by **Richard Templar**
This is a great book to read cover to cover, and there are a handful of chapters that will help your communication skills. A couple of standout chapters are 'Your attitude influences their response' and 'Earn their respect'.

- *The Dictionary of Body Language* by **Joe Navarro**
In 407 concise points, this book illustrates some general meanings behind our body language, which normally speaks more than our words do.

Mental Health

Mental health refers to your psychological and emotional well-being. Your emotional well-being is going to be really important during this time, because not only is a wedding an emotionally-charged event, it is for most of us, the biggest event we ever have in our lives. Because of this relatively rare combination, your mental health during this time might be something you want to take extra care of.

Depending on who you are, your wedding planning period may or may not be full of emotions. Some couples are easy-going and the process is a breeze for them. For others, there are plenty of emotions flying, all kinds of positive and negative ones. If you are in the latter group, and all the emotions that you experience during your wedding planning period don't have a regular outlet, the emotional pressure can build up inside you and may just burst out in an unexpected manner. Even if you are generally good at managing your emotional state, extra care during this time might be helpful, as a measure of prevention.

Think about Mr Big in the first *Sex and the City* movie. If you haven't seen it, it goes a little like this (spoiler alert): the first half of the movie centres around planning the wedding of Carrie and Mr Big. What was initially supposed to be a small wedding began to grow in size, and this was starting to concern Mr Big. He let the concerns and emotional pressure build up without releasing the valve or talking to his partner, Carrie. When the day finally came and the moment to get married was upon him, he panicked and didn't get out of the wedding car at the ceremony. The pressure got too much. He is made out to be the bad guy in this moment, but actually, this is exactly how a wedding can get too much for you. That is, if you don't release the pressure enough throughout the wedding planning period.

Mental health is something that is unique to everyone, because it's on the inside of us. What my mental health is will be different to your mental health, which will be different to your friend's mental health, etc. Since it is so personal, I am going to particularly frame this chapter with my mental health experience. You may be able to relate to some elements, while others you may not. My experience will be something of an example of what may occur to you too, or maybe encompass *more* than your experience. It is not an exhaustive list of all the mental health related experiences that could happen, but, even if you can't exactly relate, you can hopefully understand that all sorts of experiences *can* occur, and this can still give you solace. At the very least, I hope I can reassure you that you are not alone in experiencing unexpected emotions, even if they are not the exact same emotions I experienced.

Your Story Brain Dump Space

My Story

This was the hardest part of the wedding planning process for me. It is a little window into the inside of my head during this period. But I have often been told I overthink things and look into things way too much. This very well may be true, but I can't help it, yet. I'm working on it. At this point, this little window is what it is, the window is in the past, and these are the facts about my feelings during that time. I am going to start with the least positive, and then work my way up the mood scale as we go on, finishing on the nicer self-care side of mental health that I knew of at the time.

The first mental hurdle was the proposal. When Luke got on one knee and proposed, I really was taken by surprise. We had already been together for 4 years. We had discussed getting married and I knew it was coming, but in the actual moment I was surprised. Knowing that something is *coming*, and knowing that something is happening *RIGHT NOW*, are 2 very different things. When I only knew that a wedding was coming, I was safe knowing that "oh yeah I'll get married in the future", because the future is a vague and non-committal measure of time. It is an 'it will happen one day' kind of mind-set. But Luke proposing to me made marriage part of my 'right now', and I was like, "Oh shit, this is really happening."

I felt a bit blind-sided really. I'm not saying this in a negative way, and some people really love the surprise anyway. But think about it: Luke had months to mentally prepare himself for being engaged. He had put thought into designing an engagement ring, saving for it, ordering it, and planning when it was going to happen so that everything lined up nicely for our little family holiday in Brisbane. I didn't have those months. It just got sprung on me, and then I had to mentally prepare for this next stage in my life *at the same time* as I was planning the wedding itself. This is one of the biggest milestones in my life, and I didn't get the time to mentally prepare myself in the same way as Luke. Nor did I get to have a say in when this milestone happened in my life. To decide, as a couple, when to be engaged—as many couples do choose to do—is a very sensible, practical choice that both halves equally get a say in. And while it's becoming more common, it's not a novel idea; my own parents became engaged in this manner 30 years ago.

It wasn't because of Luke, nor was it his fault. I loved and love him so dearly—then and now. He is my best friend and the love of my life, and I have never had a doubt about marrying him. It was about the lack of time to adjust. For the modern-day woman, who studies or works or is building her own future, the start of her engagement to a partner might be something she DOES want to have a say in. And sure, Luke didn't *have* to get on one knee and propose; we could've discussed when to become engaged, and then I would've had that time to mentally prepare. But that's a 'what if?' question I'm not even going to entertain because the fact is that is not what happened, reality did, and thinking about that route is not helpful now. We were 22 and 23 years old respectively and just following social norms for heterosexual couples. So, I do not blame Luke for my lack of mental preparedness and it is not a 'would've could've should've' situation because, even now, I would not change anything about those moments; I learnt a lot from them. I also don't believe we did not talk about it enough together because we did talk about it a lot. I just couldn't foresee my reaction to being unexpectedly proposed to because I had never been proposed to before, and had never experienced planning a wedding before. I was as surprised by my feelings as I was about the proposal.

As a result, a couple of weeks into our engagement, when all the initial hype had settled, I did panic. I was still a uni student, living at home, and I was about to become a WIFE. All the wives I knew were older than me. Becoming a wife meant entering the BIG LEAGUES of adulthood. It felt like I was about to officially become an adult, even though I was already an adult and had been for years. This moment also ended up coinciding with me officially moving out of home. So, 2 milestones were occurring. AND on top of all this, it wasn't just a move out of home, but a move to the other side of the world. 3 big milestones. Now, personal growth happens when you are outside of your comfort zone, so essentially by definition these milestones were going to make me feel a little uncomfortable, and maybe even a little nervous. That was OK, I had expected an acceptable level of uncomfortable feeling. But the wedding to me was like the master key to the doors to all 3 milestones, and it all got too much for me on a couple of occasions.

The issue I believe was just how quickly everything was changing, and I didn't give myself time to process. I went from a relatively naïve university student, still living at home with a part-time job, a boyfriend and paving the way to a couple of local job offers through work experience, to suddenly becoming engaged, getting married in less than 11 months and deciding on moving to the other side of the world shortly thereafter, to a place I had never been to, nor had any career prospects in. It was all mushed together in a short space of time, and it literally all came about in a short space of time. In the 3 months from Christmas 2016 to March 2017, my whole life re-routed its course. When my mental state caught up with my physical state, damn right did it have a little panic!

This particular series of events is all obviously very unique to me, but it's not uncommon to have multiple milestones happening around the same time as your wedding. Moving into a new home, building a house, having a baby—these are all common things that might be happening around weddings. Nor is it uncommon for women to still be proposed to in a surprising manner, so while you might happily welcome the surprise, what I wouldn't be surprised to find is that you have that mini freak out where you realise what just happened. Keep in mind, when you become engaged, it doesn't necessarily mean you're having a wedding straight away. I know a lot of friends who have become engaged and have been engaged for years, with no wedding in sight. But for the majority of engaged couples, it does mean wedding time. The fact that you suddenly have a wedding to plan for in your near future might throw off some other plans you had for your life. That happens in a relationship; things change for each other. But if you don't get a say in when exactly you want this wedding period to occur, you could potentially be a little disappointed with the change in your sequence of life events. Don't feel guilty if you've noticed this in yourself—any combination of any of these feelings is totally normal to feel.

YOUR STORY BUILDING BLOCK #21: SETTLING INTO THE IDEA OF GETTING MARRIED

How do you feel about getting married?

How are you coping with the first months of your engagement?

What have you discussed so far with your partner?

How are you feeling about your partner?

What other milestones are occurring about the same time as your wedding?

How are you feeling about your sequence of life events during this period?

What are you having to change in your life to allow for your wedding?

How do you feel about making those changes?

What's your gut feeling telling you about your upcoming marriage?

When the panic moments occurred for me—and if I recall correctly there were 2 main moments—my mum and Luke were there for me. The thing is, because these panic moments were about the wedding, it was a double-edged sword going to them for support. Whenever I feel down, I would, on a normal occasion, turn to these two people: Luke or my mum. Heck I can't hide anything from my mum anyway even when I do try; she's that kind of mum. But when it came to the wedding, they were so involved in it too, that if I was upset, as the bride, it would dampen their feelings about the wedding as well, and it made me feel worse. My being upset was upsetting them, because I was the bride and I was supposedly *supposed* to be happy. I tried to just deal with it myself a little bit, but that's why I burst on a couple of occasions. It was a bit of a catch-22. This is why I can empathise with Mr Big in *Sex and the City*. Sometimes you just don't feel like talking about what you are feeling because you feel you are likely to upset those around you and those you care about. I also didn't want to ruin the experience of the wedding for my fiancé or my mum. After all, it was Luke's wedding too and for my mum, I was her first child to get married. In hindsight, I potentially could've considered seeking out some professional help during this time. This way I could have talked more freely and to someone removed from the wedding. But this wasn't something I was aware of as an option then.

I know that for me a good cry usually helps; back then this was one of the only ways I knew would. So, on those couple of occasions, Luke and my mum were there to wipe away my tears. I don't know what it is, but I like to believe crying is my body psychologically letting go of something, by physically letting go of tears. When I get to the point of crying, this is usually my lowest point, and once I've let all the tears out, all those little drops of emotion, I breathe and calm down, and I do feel better. Even though the act of 'letting it out' like this helps, it probably didn't have to get to this if I had a more effective outlet to release all the unexpected emotions I was experiencing. The big white wedding was supposed to be this grand time filled with happy excitement and laughter and pink champagne (or so it was in the movies). The fact it was not feeling like this all of the time made me feel something was wrong with me.

Talking is a hard thing to do for a lot of people. Sometimes it is because we don't want to admit things, and other times we are afraid of making ourselves vulnerable and exposing something that, we think in the wrong hands, could be turned around and used against us. Sometimes what we need to talk about feels embarrassing to say out loud. Sometimes it is for selfless reasons like we don't want to upset or bother others, as mentioned earlier. Sometimes there are other reasons. Back then, I never used to talk the way I do now. Luke comes from a family who talks more openly about feelings, and from the minute we started dating he tried to encourage me to talk to him. It wasn't until 2 years into our relationship that I really started to feel comfortable and trust him enough to open up, and from then on, I haven't been able to shut up. Back to the wedding; after a couple of initial emotional panicky bursts, I had reached a place where I was comfortable opening up to Luke and my mum, even if it was uncomfortable. And I am very grateful for having had them, because I have no idea how I would've reacted if I didn't have someone to unload to. My mum got most of my tears though, with Luke in New Zealand and me living mostly at home with my parents. Sorry mum.

The thing I found hard talking to mum and Luke, aside from the fact that I thought it would upset them, was the fact that they thought they needed to provide me the answers to my problems. This is not necessarily why you talk to someone. Sure, there are instances where by talking through an issue with someone else and asking their opinion, you actually do get a different perspective from them and feel better. Maybe you even went to them specifically for advice because they have been through what you are going through, or have more experience in a particular area. But they don't *have* to provide this. Sometimes you just **want someone to listen**. My mum has always just wanted her children to be safe and happy, so will try her hardest to help if we are not either of those things. Luke is the same; if he knows I am unhappy, he will try and 'fix it'. I understand this, because I can feel the same in reverse sometimes. If I know those around me are unhappy, especially those closest to me like my mum or my now-husband, I feel there's a sense of care and duty I have to help them become happy again. I care for them and their well-being. But sometimes, when we think we're helping, we end up actually making things worse. Sometimes, the best thing to do is to do nothing but listen, even if doing nothing makes you feel like you have done nothing. Truth is, it doesn't matter how you feel. It's about how the other person who is talking feels. It's about what they need in those moments. And if they need you to just listen, and if they have felt heard by you doing nothing

133

but listening, then actually you *have* done something. I know that, when this is me, when I need to talk and let things out, all I need is someone to rant to.

This is what being supportive is: **being the *type* of support someone needs at any one time.** If it's just an ear someone needs, then just be an ear. If they want your advice on what to do, then provide suggestions. So—here is my TIP—communicate to the people closest to you what *type* of support you need at any given time. While this took a bit of practice, over the time since my wedding this has worked really well from my experience, even with people who I thought it would be hard to do so with.

YOUR STORY BUILDING BLOCK #22: SOMEONE TO TALK TO

How do you feel about talking to others?

Who could you talk to regularly to unload during this time?

Who do you trust?

Who provides you with great support, when you need it?

How can you communicate to those closest to you, how you would like to be supported?

What happens if this person is unavailable?

Who is not a great person for you to unload to?

If you don't like talking, what other ways are there to unload your feelings and release the emotional pressure?

Something else I struggled to talk about and deal with when it came to the wedding—actually more so the marriage this time—was my surname change. I was not cool with having to change my surname. But I come from a family of female name-changers and I was struggling to find someone to discuss this with to get to a solution. Only heterosexual females seem to have to face this. I find this an unfair imposition on a heterosexual bride (I go into this more in the later chapter <u>Traditions and Generation Gaps</u>). I was just expected to either change my name—my *NAME*—that I have had for 20 plus years, plus go through all the admin involved with organising that change. Or, I keep my name, which I was surprised to find was going to cause more disappointment than I thought it would.

I wanted to keep my name. But I also wanted to have the same surname as my husband and my future children. That to me is the whole point of a surname, to unite your family. But in order to do this, I had to change my surname, which I didn't want to do. Luke was not even considering the possibility of changing his own surname to mine, because that is not the norm in our culture. And it is obviously easier for me to change mine; it is the more expected option and I am the one who has been conditioned my entire life to change my surname. I am the one who had been supposedly 'mentally prepared' for this choice, whereas Luke would've needed the time to mentally get there. In that sense, it is similar to the surprise element of the proposal and being mentally prepared for a marriage.

This decision was rolling about in my head the whole wedding planning period, and for months post-wedding. I was trying to blend my stance on gender equality, with sharing the same surname in our new little family Luke and I were creating with this marriage. There was this inner conflict inside me, and this caused so much anxiety on its own. There were a couple of tears on this issue too. In the end, it took me a year and a half into our marriage to actually legally change my surname to my husband's. But my compromise was this: Morelli, my first surname, was going to become my middle name. By accident, I had never legally had a middle name, so here it is. And, I can assure you, the initial M. will always be presented in my name: Juliet M. Dujmovic.

Even if you are all for changing your surname to your partner's, it does take a while to get used to. Depending on your lifestyle, there is a lot of admin that you need to organise to change your surname everywhere. In places like the UK, using different surnames for different household bills, banks, etc. can affect your credit rating, so you'll want to make sure you have changed your name EVERYWHERE. It will take a while to get used to using and saying your new name, but from my experience there is a bit of a transition period; I am in the middle of this right now, as I am writing these words. Some places I use my new name and other places I do not. I still use the email with my old surname in it, as well as my new email with my new surname in it. After all my resistance to the change, I am not surprised it is taking me forever to properly adopt my new name full-time.

If you are dealing with a surname change for your wedding, take the practicalities of your surname change as it comes, and change over to your new name at your own pace. In the public arena, I have experienced no judgement at all on this; when I explained to a bank that I was changing my surname, albeit almost 2 years after the marriage, not an eyelash was bashed. It seems a transition period is acceptable in the world of surname changes for women (dare I say *only* women though?). There's also no need to rush it. You don't need to change your name as soon as possible after the wedding. You can mull over the move for as long as you need.

What have you and your partner decided to do in regards to surnames?

How do you feel about your decision?

How much time will you take to change your surname post-wedding?

How much of this decision is truly yours?

How are other people around you influencing your decision?

What could help to make you feel better about your decision?

Who can you talk to, to get some advice?

Another tradition that was causing me anxiety was the Hen's night/Bachelorette party for me and the Buck's night/Bachelor party/stag do for Luke. Whatever you call them in your country, they stereotypically involve drinking and a stripper. I did not want a stripper. I did not want Luke to have a stripper. Luke did not want a stripper either, and he did not want me having a stripper. I was so uncomfortable about it. I have nothing against the profession; I just don't feel comfortable with this event in the wedding procedures being treated like 'the last night out as a single person'. FYI, just because you are not married yet, does not mean you are single; Luke and I were still boyfriend-girlfriend, and fiancés. Some of the things I have seen for myself or have heard from men close in my life that happen on these nights, on any other day of the year is cheating. If you are cool with that that's fine; that's your choice and if you are happy then I respect that. Both Luke and I were not, and that choice needed to rest with us, for *our* wedding. We asked both sides of our bridal party not to give us this entertainment, but I was still anxious about this in the lead up to this night, because this kind of entertainment is usually 'a surprise' and not always in your own control.

Extra wedding events like these are typical for Western weddings, but also for other cultures too. I have been part of weddings that have cultural or religious events in the week leading up to a wedding, and this might be the case for you. Sometimes you don't have a choice as to whether you have the events or not; you just do. And just because you have a certain extra wedding event, doesn't necessarily mean you agree with it. These events might still cause you anxiety, nerves, or uncomfortable feelings. Usually, I have found, these events aren't actually organised by you or your partner; they're organised by your family, your bridal party, your friends, etc. Have a private 1-on-1 discussion early on with the relative parties, and just relay to them the parts you aren't comfortable with. Talking this through with them can help, and the fact that you are having the conversation in private can also help them take it more seriously. If 1-on-1 is not comfortable for you, then maybe ask a trusted person who understands your stance to be present for the conversation. The parts of your wedding that are making you uncomfortable can be potentially left out or compromised on. Maybe even opening up to other people who have been through the events you aren't comfortable with might reveal that you are not the only one in your family or friends circle that has experienced your feelings. Knowing you have someone to relate to so closely can really help, and together you might even be able to cause some change.

YOUR STORY BUILDING BLOCK #24: ADDITIONAL WEDDING EVENTS

What wedding-related events are causing you concern?
What could you do to reduce these feelings?

Who can you talk to about the parts of these wedding-related events?

Who is in control of these wedding-related events?

How can you approach these people so that they best understand how these events are making you feel?

Aside from the emotions that dealt with logistics and traditions, there are other emotions directly related to planning a big event. It is naturally overwhelming to organise a big event. As I've mentioned a couple of times now, a wedding is for most people the biggest event they have, and there are a lot of moving parts. For Luke and I, this overwhelm was made even bigger by the short 11-month engagement period we had to plan our wedding in. Stress levels were high, and this can always affect your mental health.

Planning a big event, with all the moving parts, has lots of communication and confrontation. Events like this need people to be proactive, make decisions efficiently and take a bit of a lead. For our wedding, I was able to do this, and our parents were able to do this. Our parents took the main lead during the times Luke and I were both in New Zealand, which was then reassigned to me when I got back to Adelaide. Basically, I had all the information, so if anyone needed to know something, they would ask me. I was the call centre for the wedding. If I needed to ask people to do something, I was comfortable asking them to, and I was comfortable talking with the wedding coordinator and suppliers directly. The parents were also comfortable doing these two things, so if I couldn't, I could trust that they would step up to the plate. Throughout the year we all got little tasks that we managed individually as well. For example:

- My father-in-law took charge on organising a coffee machine and coffee maker

- My mother-in-law took charge of cleaning all of our wedding rings for the day
- My dad took charge of making the little wooden name placements for the engagement party
- My mum took charge of organising food for the morning of, before the ceremony
- Etc.

This is not an exhaustive list, but you get the idea. It really was a collaborative experience, and everyone took the lead when they needed to. We had our little team.

But not everyone is like this. Talking to people, or being confrontational to negotiate or request a discount for damaged goods is not everyone's cup of tea. Some people don't like taking the lead, and prefer to be led instead. That is absolutely fine, but it may cause a lot more stress to you and those around you while you are planning your wedding. Part of this is being organised, feeling calm and keeping on top of everything, and the second part is being able to communicate effectively. I found if I had these 2 things, everything else mostly fell into place. Still, there were a couple of times where I wish I had been more confident and spoken up more, like when speaking to my rogue wedding vendor. I have accepted this as a lesson learnt for me—I just needed some more growing.

YOUR STORY BUILDING BLOCK #25: TAKING THE LEAD

How do you feel about taking the lead on a project?

How can you split the leadership role with your partner?

On a scale from 1 to 10, where 1 is definitely a follower and 10 is definitely a leader, where do you think you sit when it comes to leading?

How can you use this as an opportunity to grow?

What is causing you the most concern about leading and being proactive?

What will you need help with?

How do you feel about asking people for things and potentially being confrontational?

Who do you trust with taking the lead on different tasks?

Who can you rely on to get a job done?

Who are you most concerned about getting to do some work?

Who is someone you could talk to whose leadership skills you admire?

When can you see this person?

Poor mental health shows up in your life in funny little ways. Despite being typically 'invisible' to anyone other than yourself, it can still manifest in physical tell-tale signs. These physical signs differ from person to person, and also between different times in your life. For example, let's look at stress. I know that my body responds to stress in physical ways. I first learnt this when I was 20 years old and had taken on way too many commitments. For the first time in my life, I was stretched thin and experienced what stress *really* felt like for me. I unintentionally lost 10kgs in a month, and that was a sign from my body telling me I needed to say 'no' to a few things. Fast forward to the wedding planning period, which was coinciding with the end of my university degree, my eye sight started deteriorating. I could not look at some text without it becoming unfocused and I needed to blink a lot. The optometrist confirmed this was most likely due to stress, with so many big things going on, and all I could do was monitor it. Sure enough, this issue disappeared post-wedding. I also had 4 colds during those 11 months, which is ridiculously high for my usual health levels; 2 of those colds coincided with our engagement party and the ladies high tea we had. I do not believe for a second that this was a coincidence, because it is very much a trend in my life. When I've been super busy organising something, the event comes around, everything is done and I can finally relax and let my guard down, BAM a cold rushes in. I tried to arrange everything so that not too much was happening all at the same time—engagement party, graduation, etc.—but it was still a very busy and full-on 11-months, and it took its little toll.

So, when my body starts to give me signs of stress, I know I need to do something about it, just like when I was 20 years old and needed to start saying 'no'. Being organised plays a huge part in reducing stress levels, for 2 reasons. On the one hand, things that are organised are under control; there is a sense of calm, not chaos. And on the other hand, being organised, in the context of a wedding, means things are in order and on time, *which means* things are happening, *which means* the number of things you need to do for the wedding is going down. I will emphasise though, that while being organised plays a big part, it's not the only contributing factor. Even though I believe I am an organising queen, and organised our wedding extremely well, it was not enough; I was still experiencing stress. Who knows what I would've been like had I not been organised? It would've been a lot worse, so keeping organised will help a lot. At the very least, being organised will actually unlock more free time for you to focus on taking care of yourself better, especially as it gets closer to your wedding day, which is a double win.

YOUR STORY BUILDING BLOCK #26: MENTAL HEALTH IN PHYSICAL SIGNS

How does poor mental health physically manifest in your life?

How do you know when your mental state is in a healthy place?

What signs does your body give you when you are stressed?

How do YOU know when you have met your absolute stress limit?

What other signs are there in your thoughts, words or behaviour?

What has helped in the past to reduce these physical manifestations?

What new measures could you try to help keep your mental state healthy?

Think back to the question in Building Block #21, asking what other milestones are occurring about the same time as your wedding. How can you arrange everything so that you don't have too many things happening at one time?

What would balance in your life look like for you during this period?

How can you find this balance?

To combat all the overwhelming stress, anxiety, guilt, internal conflict… and all the other emotions that were coming up, I tried to keep the self-care and self-love up, what I knew it to be at that time. Mental health and self-care often go hand in hand these days. Like 2 little friends holding hands and skipping along.

The first self-care element I'm going to mention is your physical health. I'm talking fitness, diet and exercise. If I had eaten healthier and exercised more regularly—2 basic parts to good physical health—I just might not have had as many colds as I did, and probably would've handled my stress better. This will probably alter from person to person, but it is a known fact that taking care of your physical health positively impacts your mental health as well. I happened to actually test this fact during my wedding planning period (unintentionally but a happy and useful accident nonetheless). I had an unexpected surgery during my wedding planning period which took 4 months to heal, during which I wasn't allowed to do much physical activity. Despite the reduction in my usual levels of physical activity, I didn't stop putting the same amount of food in my mouth! When you keep eating what you've always eaten, even when you suddenly stop moving as much, take it from me it catches up to you. For me it resulted in some weight gain, and my mum literally had me join a gym for the last month leading up to our wedding to ensure the wedding dress fit me in the same way it had when we had ordered it. Alterations were done already and it was too late to change the fit, so I had to change the bride. Not only did I do regular exercise, but my diet was monitored and I adopted a healthier eating plan. Despite being the last month before the wedding—and probably the busiest month getting last minute items done and all the wedding events also occurring in this month, junk food and alcohol included—it was the best that I had felt in a while. The test had worked. In hindsight I definitely could have increased my attention to my health a lot earlier in the wedding planning process, at the very least my diet, had I truly understood the impact it was going to have on my overall mood and ability to cope with everything. It is common for brides to try and intentionally lose weight for their wedding, and if this is you that is fine. The added bonus for you will be that taking care of your physical health is going to positively impact your mental health during a typically stressful time. But even if you aren't looking to lose weight for your wedding, engaging in a healthy lifestyle and giving some attention to this area will be a great help.

YOUR STORY BUILDING BLOCK #27: HEALTH

How is your health?

What can you do to ensure a healthy diet during this wedding period?

What can you do to ensure enough physical exercise to combat stress?

What are you already doing that makes you feel good about your health?

What changes can you make to your routine to encourage a healthier lifestyle?

How might you wish to continue this post-wedding?

Now for the self-love. Self-love is, quite literally, love for your Self, so it is totally personal and can mean anything from brushing your teeth to a total weekend of all your favourite things. When we love, we care, so loving yourself easily translates into caring for yourself.

YOUR STORY BUILDING BLOCK #28: SELF-LOVE

How do you love yourself?

How do you care for yourself day to day?

What are your favourite self-love activities?

What are some self-love activities that you'd like to try?

For me, I reeeaallly love a good massage. I could happily have them weekly if my budget allowed. Since it does not, a massage is a special treat I like to give myself at least once a year. For our wedding planning period, I decided a couple of massages would do. From the second I got engaged, I knew I wanted a spa day for all the bridesmaids, my mum, my mother-in-law, and myself. About a month before the wedding, we had a lovely morning filled with massages, manicures and pedicures, followed by a Chinese restaurant banquet. This way all the ladies could have a morning to relax. Straight after the wedding, I also had a massage just with my mum. This was a little mother and daughter date before I moved away, but also a post-wedding treat to thank ourselves for all our hard work. These were the little rewards for those involved; something to look forward to, to relax and just pause for a few hours.

Now, I wasn't consciously doing the above as 'self-care' activities. I just love massages and relaxing. Who doesn't love relaxing? And relaxing means different things to different people. But, today, after a few years of personal development and life coaching, I am much more aware of the importance of having a self-care routine.

Now, so many of us are familiar with the 'but first, coffee' style statements; one must get their cup of coffee first in the morning, in order to function properly. Self-love is the same; one must get their daily dose in order to function properly. So, I have developed the Cup of Self-Love. This can apply to everyday life, but also particularly for your wedding planning period.

Cup of Self-Love

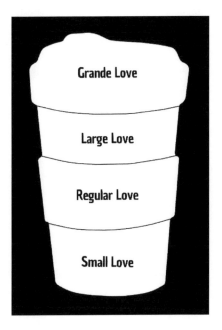

The Cup of Self-Love is based on coffee cup sizes, so that will help you remember it. And it's a reusable cup of course, because we're environmentally-friendly here, and the self-love activities are also reusable.

The basis for your Cup of Self-Love is that you need to keep it filled. At the bottom, we have Small Love activities. These are activities that you can do on a daily basis, and take anywhere from 10 minutes to an hour to engage in.

The Regular Love activities are ones you do on a weekly to monthly basis, so not as often as the daily Small Love. But, these are the ones you can devote a bit more time to—an hour to a few hours.

The Large Love are the bigger ones, which might take a bit

more preparation; maybe even cost a bit more. Because they are bigger, you engage with them less, say, every month, every 3 months, or up to a couple of times a year. They can be anywhere from a few hours to a whole day or two.

The Grande Love is for the devotees to their Self-Love and Personal Development. These are the activities that you might do once every 1 or 2 years, but can be anywhere from a day to a month long.

If you like the Cup of Self-Love, then you can fill in your own in the Bonus Material section. As the quote goes, "you can't pour from an empty cup", so fill up your Cup and drink from it daily, just like your morning coffee.

Your Self-Love activities are totally up to you. What might be a Large Love activity for some, might be a Small or Regular activity for others. It's completely personal. To help get your creative thought-process going, here's a list of activities that can fill your Cup. You may already be engaging with some of them:

- Taking care of your general hygiene (brushing your teeth, having a shower, brushing your hair, etc.)
- Giving yourself a little extra boost just because (doing your hair nicely, wearing make-up, wearing a nice outfit or nice underwear)
- Having a cup of tea or coffee by yourself
- Waking up a little earlier before everyone else does, and have that quiet time to yourself
- Cooking and baking
- Doing some of your favourite hobbies or activities (reading, going for a run)
- Trying some mindfulness hobbies (colouring in, tapestry or sewing, painting, drawing, lighting a candle)
- Doing exercise (going to the gym, joining a sports club,

swimming, running)
- Yoga or meditation
- Religious or spiritual activities
- Working on your personal development (doing a course, learning a new skill)
- Holidays and retreats

What other self-love activities can you think of?

Something else that is super important to your self-care during this time is time alone with your partner. Kind of like a pre-wedding honeymoon. The whole point of a honeymoon is to spend time alone with your partner to enjoy being married and relax after all the wedding hype. This is just as important before the wedding, if not even more so. When you are in the process of planning your wedding, with emotions flying high, tasks to be done and things happening all around, it is more important than ever to remember what it is all for, and that is you and your partner. For us, this sort of just happened, because when I visited Luke in New Zealand, it was just the two of us, and we got to spend some really special quality time together. When we were together, we were separated by an ocean from everyone else and all the wedding stuff. I really enjoyed and appreciated these times in New Zealand throughout the year; they were my deep breathes in between all of the running around in Australia. Obviously, not everyone has a country to escape to while they are planning their wedding. It just has to be time alone with your partner—regular date nights, a day out together, etc. These will do just fine. But if you want, and if it is possible for you, you can definitely make it bigger by having a pre-wedding honeymoon or going away for little weekend trips.

Most importantly, use some of these moments together to keep the care and support alive between you and your partner pre-wedding. It can be pretty stressful and emotional in the lead-up, so check in with your partner regularly, make sure they're doing ok, and voice your appreciation for the work they're doing towards your wedding. A lot of people plan for their wedding in their free time, around full-time work and other commitments. It can get busy and exhausting, but when it feels appreciated and is acknowledged, it tends to be easier to do. So, thank your partner for their efforts, show your appreciation, and ensure they are coping internally with the upcoming marriage. Don't feel afraid to ask your partner to reciprocate these acknowledgements as well. It's ok to ask your partner this; not everyone knows how many times you want to be asked, "How are you going with everything?". Your partner deserves to know what you need and how to support you. While you may wish to, this doesn't necessarily mean divulging information that might upset your partner—as discussed already, maybe you wish to talk to qualified professionals, who are removed from the wedding. But we can still check in and see if they are ok. So, show a little extra appreciation and care for each other during this more emotional time.

YOUR STORY BUILDING BLOCK #29: QUALITY TIME WITH YOUR PARTNER

How often are you getting quality time alone with your partner?

How often would you like to be getting quality time alone with your partner?

How can you make this a priority during this wedding planning period?

What kind of activities would you like to do with your partner?

How open are you with your partner?

How open is your partner with you?

What are your partner's main concerns and worries with the upcoming marriage?

How often do you wish to be checked in with by your partner?

How often does your partner wish to be checked in with?

In what ways do you wish to show your appreciation of your partner?

How can you acknowledge the efforts your partner is going to?

How do you feel about asking your partner to reciprocate extra appreciation and care during this time?

Finally, the night before the wedding, my last little self-care moment was planned. I drew myself a bath. It was late, everyone had gone to bed and it was nice and quiet. I could've gone to bed too for an extra hour of sleep, but I had a bath instead. It was just a private moment by myself, with a nice smelling bath bomb in the water. It really was the pause to catch up with myself and just take in what was actually going to happen the next day. Up until this point it had all been so surreal, and it still was really. I just sat there thinking, "this is the last night before I become a married woman", and I let that float around in my head (pun intended).

The thing about self-care is that you mostly do it alone. Activities alone don't always register as a high priority task for some people. I didn't have to have that bath; I could've had that extra hour of sleep. I was getting up at 5am, so sleep could easily have been a higher priority. But I made an appointment with myself that night, to have a bath. If I had made an appointment with any other person, I would have shown up. An appointment with myself is no different. For weeks, I had it in my mind that I would like a bath the night before our wedding. I had bought the bath bomb especially for it. So, it didn't matter that it was late; I needed to show up, and that bath meant more to me than that potential extra hour of sleep. I was running on adrenaline the next day anyway, so I didn't miss the sleep at all. But that bath was the last bath before I got married, I remember it as clear as day and I am quite grateful for that bath.

YOUR STORY BUILDING BLOCK #30: SELF-LOVE APPOINTMENTS

When can you make appointments with yourself to do some of these self-love activities?

How regularly can you make this occur for your wedding planning period?

Who else close to you might also need some self-love during this time?

How can you support each other in your self-love activities?

The Wedding Day and Beyond

For the wedding day itself, funnily enough, all brides I've spoken to, including myself, were incredibly calm. Everything that had led up to this wedding day, all the preparing, organising, stressing, all the feelings and all the money, it had all been for this day. It was time to enjoy what all the hard work was for. And it seems the majority of brides are actually not Bridezillas, contrary to popular belief.

For me, I would've been more anxious and stressed if I had not been fully prepared for the day. In the lead up to the wedding I did everything in my power to avoid this situation. I've already mentioned how being organised plays a big part of stress, and in the Practical Bits chapter I detailed how you can organise and prepare for your wedding day, particularly the 'Wedding Day Survival Kit'. To briefly detail this again, this was just a zip up bag that had anything and everything that we might need on the day. The answers to all the 'what if [this] happens?' questions, we basically put in a bag, just so all those little things would be covered and would not cause Luke or myself any additional little stresses. It was a bag that gave us peace of mind. Check out the Bonus Material section in Practical Bits again to see the list of potential items for a 'Wedding Day Survival Kit'.

I'm now going to take this moment to talk to you about sex on your wedding night. As the traditional saying goes—no sex until you're married—sex and marriage go hand in hand for some couples. This tradition might not be as strictly upheld as it used to be, but it still happens. It is particularly common for parents, who are from those stricter times, to like to believe this is the case either way, so once a wedding has happened then they feel they don't have to tiptoe around the issue anymore. I want to give some attention to this, because if you are a woman who is planning to have sex for the first time on your wedding night, this could be another anxiety causer.

First of all, you're going to be so tired by the night of your wedding; just have a good sleep. Second: ok, so you're married and can have sex now. Technically, you don't actually *have* to have sex on your wedding night; it's just the first night that you *could* have sex. Knowing that it is expected of you to have sex on your wedding night can make it feel planned and unnatural. You might even feel funny knowing that those around you *know* you've just had sex for the first time. There's nothing stopping you from waiting a couple of nights, when you feel more refreshed and comfortable, and can actually take the time to enjoy it or let it come about naturally. Engage and speak to your partner about this. If your partner is not a woman, they might also not understand that sex for the first time can potentially be painful for a woman, and that you don't really want to finish your wedding day like that if it is. Maybe you weren't expecting that either, and might even feel a little wounded from the experience. If you're excited to have sex for the first time on your wedding night then that is absolutely fine, go nuts guys. Just be aware of what to expect, especially as a woman. Sex is—obviously—a 2-person job, so whatever you choose to do, talk to your partner. Married now or not, communicate before, during and after sex. Speak up if something is uncomfortable or hurting, and speak up if you want the pace to go slower. If you want to do little bits at a time, say so. Speak up if you want to stop. Ladies take longer to naturally lube up for sex, so don't go forcing anything in there too fast. And have toilet paper nearby because it can be messy. Sex is not like they do it in the movies; you don't just roll over and sleep. There's wiping and catching stuff and tying condoms and all sorts. And ladies, save a pee for after sex to help flush out any bacteria that might have got in the urinary tract.

YOUR STORY BUILDING BLOCK #31: FIRST SEX ON YOUR WEDDING NIGHT

How are you feeling about having sex for the first time?

How are you feeling about having sex for the first time ON your wedding night?

How comfortable are you discussing this with your partner?

What will help to make you feel more comfortable about discussing this?
Who else might you like to talk to?
When can you talk to your partner or someone else about this?
How can you change the situation in a way that will make you feel more comfortable?

And, lastly, I have already spoken about a pre-wedding honeymoon, but the post-wedding honeymoon is truly the point where all is said and done and you can finally, FINALLY, relax completely and reflect on what has just happened. Even if it is just a night or 2, even if it is at the local hotel, who cares? Just take that time to enjoy quality time alone with your partner. Luke and I didn't really plan a honeymoon, because we were moving to London 3 weeks after the wedding. We had planned to do a bit of tourist-y stuff when we first arrived, and then set ourselves up to live there. But a couple of things happened by accident that enabled us to relax and get the honeymoon feelings.

Because Luke and I had our wedding at a hotel, after the wedding night, we were gifted with a couple of extra nights at the hotel. This was good not only to enjoy hotel life together post-wedding, but it allowed us to take a deep breath alone, just the two of us, and let the reality of what had just happened sink in. We were married! (TIP: If you can have your wedding at a hotel venue, there are some great advantages. As well as being able to stay put and not worry about transport at the end of your wedding, another added bonus of having your wedding reception in a hotel was you and your bridal party can head to your rooms before the reception, take your shoes off, have a few drinks and freshen up. We got to do this, and it was particularly great since it was a hot day and boy did we need a few drinks! This way, the whole bridal party got a chance to breathe and enjoy the moment too. You don't want to rush through your wedding day and miss these moments to soak everything up and just enjoy!)

Prior to the big move to London, we also decided to have a few nights in Brisbane, back where it all started. This actually happened by accident—we had credit from a refunded flight ticket that we needed to use up—but, in hindsight, it was a very happy accident. Since we had been to Brisbane a few times already, we knew our way around. It wasn't a holiday where we did tourist-y things; we really just took 4 days to shop, read books, and relax. We spent those days just enjoying each other as husband and wife for the very first time, and it just helped us slow down and enjoy what an amazing moment in our lives we were living.

YOUR STORY BUILDING BLOCK #32: WEDDING AND BEYOND

How can you incorporate moments to breathe throughout your wedding day, for you and your partner, for your bridal party, etc.?

How are you taking a moment to breathe with your partner post-wedding, to soak up the beginning of your marriage?

What are you doing for your honeymoon?

If a honeymoon is not an option, what could you do instead?

Suggestion Box

1. BREATHE AND PAUSE.

Have moments to literally pause, stop everything and just breathe. This is a big milestone, and it's ok to feel overwhelmed by it. It's ok to not feel ready for it; it's usually going through the things we are not ready for that make us grow in life. So these feelings are completely normal; it's just a matter of breathing through it. You may even like to join a meditation class, or engage in some self-love talk, to let yourself know it's ok. Taking deep breaths is one of the most grounding things we can do, so if you are feeling things are getting too much, pause, step aside and breathe. Give yourself that time to process.

2. FIND SOMEONE TO TALK TO.

This I highly recommend. Whether it is a family member, your partner, a friend, or a therapist, find someone who you can really unload to, and someone who you can access regularly. This helped me a lot and I do not know what I would've done without someone to talk to. I may have burst in a way I would not have liked, and ended up regretting it. I definitely held back though, and could've unloaded more regularly. Bottling up your emotions is unlikely to ever end well, so find someone who you can totally open up to without feeling guilty. If talking is something you just don't feel comfortable doing, find another means of relieving the pressure. You could write and unload in a journal, or even join an exercise class where you can physically unload on a punching bag!

3. TAKE CARE OF YOUR HEALTH.

By health here I mean your diet and your physical activity. Some brides like to lose weight for their wedding anyway, but aside from this fact, taking care of your physical activity and diet will actually have huge impacts on your mental state and help you deal with stress better. If you are already in a great healthy routine, good, keep it up. If you are not, I highly recommend finding something that can work for you during this period. Some options could be:

- Joining a gym
- Walking regularly with a family member/friend (this can combine with point no. 2 and could be your talking time!)
- Committing to being the dog-walker each day
- Daily yoga videos on YouTube
- Signing up to a boot camp or a different exercise class
- Seeing a nutritionist
- Seeing your doctor
- Bridal party bonding on a hike

There are so many different ideas out there! But, seriously, if I could do my wedding over again, this would be something I would like to have done differently. So, learn from my mistakes.

4. KEEP ORGANISED AND BE PROACTIVE.

I usually find, both personally and for other people, that when we have so much to do in such little time —like in the moment where we have left too many things to the last minute —that is when we are most likely to panic. Keeping organised and being proactive to me is avoiding this situation. Keeping organised is creating order out of all the chaos, and being proactive is taking action and getting things done. If you keep organised and are proactive, there will be a sense of control over the situation and therefore you will feel calmer about it. If something were to go wrong, because you have been organised and proactive so far, you will have plenty of time to fix it and you can continue to be calm. Keeping organised and being proactive will go a long way in helping your stress levels. If you know this is an area you are not great in, then be honest and proactive in seeking out someone to help you. Revisit <u>Practical Bits</u> again for information on keeping organised.

5. ENGAGE IN SOME SELF-CARE AND SELF-LOVE.

This can be anything, from having that daily half an hour to yourself to have a cup of tea or read a book, to going for a massage or having a spa day. This could also be combined with point no. 3 and going for a daily run, or you could treat yourself and enjoy a really lovely healthy meal, because taking care of your physical health is also self-love. Basically, any self-care or self-love activity is something that is caring or loving yourself, taking care of your mental state and taking care of YOU. It can be anything that benefits YOU or makes YOU feel good. Whatever that something is, I recommend engaging in it regularly during this wedding planning period. You can have different activities too: it can be a small daily activity, like that cup of tea or 10-minute morning meditation, a bigger activity weekly, like a bath or a night with friends, and a big self-love activity that you do monthly or even every few months, like a massage or a weekend retreat/mini holiday.

6. HAVE QUALITY TIME ALONE WITH YOUR PARTNER (AND CHILDREN IF YOU HAVE THEM!).

I can't emphasise this enough. This is so important. Out of the 11 months of our engagement, I spent a total of 4 months in New Zealand alone with Luke, and I treasure that time so much. We really needed them, not just because we were doing the long-distance thing but because it was time away from the wedding, from the phone calls and meetings and appointments. It was time where we could go out for dinner and NOT talk about the wedding. Try and get regular alone time with your partner, and children, too, if you have them. Children were not part of my wedding planning experience but they may be part of yours, so quality time with them may also be something you will like to ensure happens.

7. CREATE A WEDDING DAY SURVIVAL KIT.

This saved us on the day. Not only did I prepare one for myself, but I did put a few things inside my bridesmaids' clutches for them as well. I like to call it 'insurance' for the day: you might not need them, but you also might, and if you do, they are ready to go. They are there for your peace of mind. If some of the smaller things go wrong, you know you have got a backup plan to cover them. Check out the Bonus Section in chapter <u>Practical Bits</u> for ideas to build up your survival kit, to give you inspiration for what items you might want in your own survival kit.

8. COME UP WITH A PANIC PLAN.

You might want to have a plan to deal with unexpected moments of panic. One common exercise to deal with anxiety or panic, is a 5-4-3-2-1 exercise. It goes something like the following:

> Name 5 things you can see
> Name 4 things you can hear
> Name 3 things you can feel
> Name 2 things you can smell
> Name 1 thing you can taste

Maybe you would like to personalise this to yourself more —maybe you would like to touch 3 different textures instead —or maybe you have a different technique to calm you down that works better. Maybe it's just taking 7 deep breathes. Whichever way you go, make sure you have a way to help you in these moments. This is an invisible item you can add to that Wedding Day Survival Kit. Have a look online for more exercise ideas that might appeal to you as well.

9. IT IS ONLY ONE DAY.

Growing up, your wedding is celebrated as 'the best day of your life'. How much pressure does that put on this single day!! And it is *so* not true. Sure, it was a really great day, but I would say it was more a marking post in my entire life, rather than the best day of my life. I would be disappointed if the best day of my life was done and over with at the age of 24. So, let's get some perspective here: it's just one day. I'm sure you are working hard and putting in a lot of effort to make this day as great as it can be, and that is all it needs to be. But it will not matter how hard you have worked, someone may still spill green mint sauce on your wedding dress (I did this accidentally to my sister-in-law on her wedding day; THANK THE HIGH HEAVENS it wiped off and was unnoticeable). If this happens to you, I would literally wager that you will be beyond the point of caring about such a little thing, and just end up laughing or brushing it aside. That is all you can do. When the day has finally arrived, anything that happens will generally be beyond your control now. Accept that things just might not go according to plan. Once you have accepted this, you will experience a sense of relief and that will be one less thing you will have to worry about!

10. KEEP THE END IN MIND.

This suggestion is Habit no. 2 of *The 7 Habits of Highly Effective People* by Stephen R. Covey. Everything you are doing, all the meetings and late nights cutting ribbon or addressing invites, all the stress… remember what it's all for. You are marrying your chosen partner. This is the end goal, and just like a marriage, it takes a little work to get there. It will all be worth it in the end, so just take it one day at a time, and keep the bigger end picture always in mind.

Summary of Questions in this Chapter

YOUR STORY BUILDING BLOCK #21: SETTLING INTO THE IDEA OF GETTING MARRIED

How do you feel about getting married?

How are you coping with the first months of your engagement?

What have you discussed so far with your partner?

How are you feeling about your partner?

What other milestones are occurring about the same time as your wedding?

How are you feeling about your sequence of life events during this period?

What are you having to change in your life to allow for your wedding?

How do you feel about making those changes?

What's your gut feeling telling you about your upcoming marriage?

YOUR STORY BUILDING BLOCK #22: SOMEONE TO TALK TO

How do you feel about talking to others?

Who could you talk to regularly to unload during this time?

Who do you trust?

Who provides you with great support, when you need it?

How can you communicate to those closest to you, how you would like to be supported?

What happens if this person is unavailable?

Who is not a great person for you to unload to?

If you don't like talking, what other ways are there to

unload your feelings and release the emotional pressure?

YOUR STORY BUILDING BLOCK #23: SURNAME CHANGE

What have you and your partner decided to do in regards to surnames?

How do you feel about your decision?

How much time will you take to change your surname post-wedding?

How much of this decision is truly yours?

How are other people around you influencing your decision?

What could help to make you feel better about your decision?

Who can you talk to, to get some advice?

YOUR STORY BUILDING BLOCK #24: ADDITIONAL WEDDING EVENTS

What wedding-related events are causing you concern?

What could you do to reduce these feelings?

Who can you talk to about the parts of these wedding-related events?

Who is in control of these wedding-related events?

How can you approach these people so that they best understand how these events are making you feel?

YOUR STORY BUILDING BLOCK #25: TAKING THE LEAD

How do you feel about taking the lead on a project?

How can you split the leadership role with your partner?

On a scale from 1 to 10, where 1 is definitely a follower

and *10 is definitely a leader, where do you think you sit when it comes to leading?*

How can you use this as an opportunity to grow?

What is causing you the most concern about leading and being proactive?

What will you need help with?

How do you feel about asking people for things and potentially being confrontational?

Who do you trust with taking the lead on different tasks?

Who can you rely on to get a job done?

Who are you most concerned about getting to do some work?

Who is someone you could talk to whose leadership skills you admire?

When can you see this person?

YOUR STORY BUILDING BLOCK #26: MENTAL HEALTH IN PHYSICAL SIGNS

How does poor mental health physically manifest in your life?

How do you know when your mental state is in a healthy place?

What signs does your body give you when you are stressed?

How do YOU know when you have met your absolute stress limit?

What other signs are there in your thoughts, words or behaviour?

What has helped in the past to reduce these physical manifestations?

What new measures could you try to help keep your mental state healthy?

Think back to the question in Building Block #21 asking what other milestones are occurring about the same time as your wedding. How can you arrange everything so that you don't have too many things happening at one time?

What would balance in your life look like for you during this period?

How can you find this balance?

YOUR STORY BUILDING BLOCK #27: HEALTH

How is your health?

What can you do to ensure a healthy diet during this wedding period?

What can you do to ensure enough physical exercise to combat stress?

What are you already doing that makes you feel good about your health?

What changes can you make to your routine to encourage a healthier lifestyle?

How might you wish to continue this post-wedding?

YOUR STORY BUILDING BLOCK #28: SELF-LOVE

How do you love yourself?

How do you care for yourself day to day?

What are your favourite self-love activities?

What are some self-love activities that you'd like to try?

YOUR STORY BUILDING BLOCK #29: QUALITY TIME WITH YOUR PARTNER

How often are you getting quality time alone with your partner?

How often would you like to be getting quality time alone with your partner?

How can you make this a priority during this wedding planning period?

What kind of activities would you like to do with your partner?

How open are you with your partner?

How open is your partner with you?

What are your partner's main concerns and worries with the upcoming marriage?

How often do you wish to be checked in with by your partner?

How often does your partner wish to be checked in with?

In what ways do you wish to show your appreciation of your partner?

How can you acknowledge the efforts your partner is going to?

How do you feel about asking your partner to reciprocate extra appreciation and care during this time?

YOUR STORY BUILDING BLOCK #30: SELF-LOVE APPOINTMENTS

When can you make appointments with yourself to do some of these self-love activities?

How regularly can you make this occur for your wedding planning period?

Who else close to you might also need some self-love during this time?

How can you support each other in your self-love activities?

YOUR STORY BUILDING BLOCK #31: FIRST SEX ON YOUR WEDDING NIGHT

How are you feeling about having sex for the first time?

How are you feeling about having sex for the first time ON your wedding night?

How comfortable are you discussing this with your partner?

What will help to make you feel more comfortable about discussing this?

Who else might you like to talk to?

When can you talk to your partner or someone else about this?

How can you change the situation in a way that will make you feel more comfortable?

YOUR STORY BUILDING BLOCK #32: WEDDING AND BEYOND

How can you incorporate moments to breathe throughout your wedding day, for you and your partner, for your bridal party, etc.?

How are you taking a moment to breathe with your partner post-wedding, to soak up the beginning of your marriage?

What are you doing for your honeymoon?

If a honeymoon is not an option, what could you do instead?

Bonus Material

Cup of Self-Love

Below is an empty template for your Cup of Self-Love. You can fill in your Cup with different activities that you would like to do at that level. Revisit this section earlier in the chapter to re-read the list of potential activities, and use that to inspire you in populating your own Cup of Self-Love.

You can find a downloadable Cup of Self-Love pdf at: www.letsgetyourlifetogether.com/bridalcoaching.

Further Reading on Mental Health

- *Overcoming Anxiety* by Helen Kennerley

This in-depth book is split into 2 parts, the first exploring the understanding of anxiety and the second providing practical strategies for managing anxiety. It is an interesting and practical read and suitable for many levels of anxiety experiences.

- *Anxiety Happens* by John P. Forsyth and Georg H. Eifert

This easy-read little book provides 52 ways to find peace of mind in a concise manner. A great little reference book and a quick read as well.

- **The digital world**

Ok, this one isn't really a further 'reading' one; it's more of a 'let's learn by doing' one. If you want to try out meditation, yoga, calming music, or something of the like, there are some amazing online resources. Youtube will be one of your best friends for this. If you have time for a 15-minute relaxing yoga session, search that. If you want a 3-hour calming nature soundtrack for an afternoon of wedding planning, search that. There's also, at the time of writing, the 31-day meditation challenge that Inner Space emails straight to your inbox, and many, many phone apps offering themselves up as meditation, fitness, and dietary companions.

Money

We all know weddings are generally not the cheapest event to plan. According to the UK Wedding Report for 2017, 40% of weddings fall between £10,000 and £20,000, with the national average being £17,913. 10% of weddings will cost more than £30,000. For Australia, the national average wedding costs $32,333 (equivalent to £17,639 at time of writing). So, it is fair to say that, for most weddings, they are likely to take a decent chunk out of the bank account (check out the reports with these statistics in the Further Reading section at the end of this chapter).

Writing this reminds me of the second episode of *Friends* season 7, 'The one with Rachel's Book'. Monica and Chandler are engaged, and have just come to realise that Monica's parents have no money to put towards their wedding. Upon seeing Monica's disappointment, Chandler offers some of his savings, which he has been saving for 6 years. But when Monica wants to spend all of it, he struggles to say yes. Monica goes on to say how this is the most special day of their lives, that she has been planning this day since she was a little girl, and that it was worth spending all Chandler's savings on. Chandler was arguing that he had saved that money for 'the future'; buying a house, having children, i.e., life after the wedding. In the end, when he explained what this future would look like, Monica decided she wanted that too, and that she was happy not spending all of his money on their wedding.

This episode basically highlights the first 2 decisions that are needed to be made when it comes to paying for a wedding:

1. Who is going to pay?

2. How much will you spend on your wedding day?

Decision number one is deciding who is going to pay and, I would also add to this, **how you are going to split the costs**, regardless of whether it is between family, parents, or between you and your partner. Even if this is an easy question, it is still worth considering as this also potentially includes how you'll be splitting costs amongst your bridal party, and how much they will contribute to costs related to them, if any.

You and your partner, or even your parents, are probably all going to have very different views on what is an appropriate amount to spend for one day, so this is decision number two.

After you have answered these 2 questions you have somewhat arrived at a budget for your wedding. Such a boundary can be really helpful in controlling your spending and give some restriction to your choices, because sometimes having too many choices can be more overwhelming than you think. Setting some restraints can also be quite helpful in ensuring you have some money set aside for 'the future', just like Monica and Chandler.

Money is something that can make people feel very overwhelmed very quickly when tracking. If the task at hand becomes too big, we are more likely to put it off. But as time goes on it gets bigger and bigger and eventually becomes too daunting to deal with, totally feeling out of your control. Money does not have to be scary, and I hope you find some tips throughout this chapter to help you manage your wedding bill better.

But, first, brain dump all your money-related wedding bits. Any budget details you already have, any concerns you have, any costs you need to remember to include, etc.

Your Story Brain Dump Space

My Story

This section lends itself very well to a question and answer structure, so that is what I've adopted here. If you *tend* to prefer a simple plan for your wedding, and not fuss too much about the details, then the following 5 questions are the main ones you'll find useful. For those who like to get into the detail, each question will have its own set of 'Your Story' Building Blocks to delve deeper and assess the detail.

Including the 2 main questions presented in the introduction of this chapter, here are the 5 main questions you'll need when it comes to paying for your wedding:

1. Who is paying and how are you splitting the costs?
2. How much will you spend on your wedding day?
3. How much are the bridal party contributing?
4. How will you manage payments?
5. How can you bring costs down?

Who is paying and how are you splitting the costs?

For almost all weddings I've been privy to the details of, the 'who' part of the paying for the wedding is usually some combination of either the couple in question or their parents. In some instances, grandparents have also contributed some funds. Traditionally in a lot of cultures, parents pay for their children's weddings. But that isn't always the case these days, with the cost of weddings and traditions progressing. Some 'children', who have focused on their careers first and in general marry later than they have in yesteryears, are in positions to pay for, or at least contribute to, their own weddings, and therefore can have greater control over where their money goes. Some choose to pay for their own weddings intentionally, even if parents offer, for a variety of reasons. Some don't have parents who are in a position to offer, and therefore have no choice. Some families might have certain family members who would like to gift the marrying couple with paying for a particular part of their wedding. There are many reasons and many different situation setups for who is paying for a wedding, but, for obvious reasons, you're going to need to know the answer to this question pretty early on.

As well as the setup for your family, you'll have to consider that of your partner's too. Maybe your partner's tradition of paying for weddings, or how their family sees it, will be different to yours. Some cultures and families believe one side of the couple pays for particular wedding items, or maybe the way they pay is different. This will depend on how similar your family's and your partner's family's cultures are, and how open they are to your own wedding proceedings and choices.

Once you know who will be involved in paying, then it's a matter of splitting the costs amongst the payers. If you and your partner are paying in full for the wedding, and already have a well-established shared life together, this may be a non-issue for you. But for others, this will be the first time you're REALLY uniting with your partner, and are wanting to consider how the costs will be split. Some couples post-marriage don't intend on joining funds, so this could be you. If parents are involved, more splitting will need to be decided on, and if those particular family members exist who want to pay for a particular wedding item, they will need to be considered too. For some families, splitting costs will be smooth and simple; for others not so much. How we communicate can make situations easier, so refer back to chapter Communication for some tips here.

If things are really difficult in your family, then it will be important early on in the process to get what you have discussed **down on paper**. "Who said they were paying for what!" arguments can be solved by referring back to notes that were taken at the time. This is how a professional would handle customer relations. While it sounds silly to take this practice up for family relations, your wedding is essentially a big project, so a lot of typically professional practices can work really well here. Have this little 'how we are splitting costs' plan and send it to all parties early on. Ensure they all see it and agree with it, and this can be used as your 'insurance' further down the track. It's hard to argue with something you've already agreed on in the past, and this little plan can help to set all expectations from the beginning. But keep it a little bit flexible; costs will pop up that you weren't expecting, and something might be cheaper/dearer than you initially budgeted for. People's circumstances can change as well during your wedding planning period, which can impact what they can afford. This can in turn impact the split, so keep this in mind, and have a think about how you'd like to work with this.

For Luke and I, our parents paid for our wedding. This was our family tradition, and our parents were in a position to do so. Luke and I were very grateful for this; there is no way we could've afforded the wedding we had if we were paying for it ourselves. I was still in university with a growing student debt, and Luke was only 6 months out of university himself. If Luke and I had to pay for our own wedding, we would have had 2 choices to consider: either have a much smaller wedding, or take out a loan.

Once we knew who was paying, how we were splitting the costs came easy after this. My parents paid for everything for me, and Luke's parents paid for everything for him. My parents paid for all the guests from our side, Luke's parents paid for all the guests from his side. For everything else, our parents went exactly

179

halves in. We didn't place exact numbers on how much each parent was paying, nor did we place exact numbers on how many items each parent was paying for. This way we kept it flexible; items were either registered as Luke-related, Juliet-related, or both-related, and split accordingly.

Something else we traditionally do in both sides of our family is pay for the bridal party as well. The alternative would be to get the bridesmaids and groomsmen to pay for themselves in full, or at least contribute to their respective dresses and suits. Either option is fine. For us, my parents paid for the bridesmaids, and Luke's parents paid for the groomsmen. They went halves on the 2 flower girls we had because we only had flower girls— no page boys—so they were present in the bridal party for both Luke and I.

YOUR STORY BUILDING BLOCK #33: WHO IS PAYING AND HOW YOU WILL BE SPLITTING THE COSTS

Who will be contributing to your wedding costs?

How are costs being split between paying parties?

How are all parties agreeing on the matter?

How will they be paying, i.e. what's their approach (pay-as-you-go, lump sum at the end, cash, bank transfer, etc.)?

When will you receive the money to pay for items?

What will you do if you do not receive money as initially agreed?

Who needs to know about your answers to these questions?

How will you agree with the people involved in paying for your wedding (verbally, in writing, etc.)?

How much will you spend on your wedding day?

There are two main factors that dictate how much you will spend on your wedding: how much you can afford and how much an average wedding costs.

The first factor depends on your 'who' will be paying:
- How much can the people paying for the wedding afford?
- How much can you and your partner afford?
- How much can your parents afford?
- Can your parents afford more/less than your partner's parents?
- How much can other contributors afford?

How much you can afford might depend on what else is going on in your life at the same time as your wedding. What other expenses, milestones or big costs do you have going on during this period? If your parents are contributing or paying for your wedding, you might find that some of them have been saving up for your wedding as you were growing up. Our parents were doing this for us. Both Luke's parents and my parents had their own personal financial plans from years ago assigning how much they would give us to pay for our wedding. But you might also find that how much your parents can afford depends on how many siblings you have. Your parents might want to spend equal amounts on each of their children. What they spend on your wedding, they'll probably want to spend equivalent on your siblings' weddings. This was the case for Luke and I. It was made very clear to us at the beginning how much each pair of parents was going to contribute for each of their children. So, the amount your wedding payers can afford is going to give you a maximum budget for your wedding.

The second factor is not necessarily something you would

pick as a factor straight away, but I found this very useful. For the brides like me who have no idea about where to even begin budgeting for your wedding, hopefully this will be useful for you too. Knowing the average costs of a wedding in your part of the world will act as a baseline to start your own estimates. For our wedding, none of us knew what an average wedding would cost in 2017; we could only guess. We thought that just guessing a number wouldn't be useful because it wouldn't be based on anything. We wanted some evidence, some estimates for costs involved in a wedding, and from there, a rough budget could be deduced. So, we basically did our wedding budget in reverse: instead of letting the budget dictate the wedding, we did some homework and let the average wedding costs dictate the budget. For example, there's no point in budgeting $100AUD for flowers from a professional florist, when your bouquet alone could cost that much!

At the very start of your wedding planning journey, it's literally impossible to know the costs of EVERYTHING. Therefore, you cannot know exactly how much it's going to cost you. Until you know exactly where you will be having your venue, what dress you are going to hire or buy, what photographer you are going to use, etc.... any budget you set from the start will be rough.

There are 2 ways you can approach the building up of your wedding budget: Bottom Up or Top Down.

Bottom Up

If you aren't on a tight wedding budget, then you might prefer this approach. Bottom Up means building up your overall budget from all the smaller rough budgets within it. Do some research to find the average costs for a wedding dress, a photographer, etc., and come up with estimates for each. Budget X amount for the wedding dress, X amount for the wedding car, X amount for the photographer, etc., and then add all of these together. This way, you're literally building up the budget from the bottom, the little building blocks of the wedding budget.

Top Down

Top Down is literally the opposite of the Bottom Up approach. This scenario is going to be most suited to those with an absolute maximum budget that will dictate all costs. The Top Down approach is to break down the budget and divide it amongst each of the areas you need to fund. Say you have X amount for the entire wedding. Maybe half of that will go towards costs for the reception, a quarter will go towards hiring photographers, florists, and the marriage ceremony, and the other quarter will go towards dressing the marrying couple and any other bits (this is totally made up do not use this as a guide! No idea if it works). Then you will have to find a reception venue that fits within that budget, etc.

Both approaches are legitimate ways of setting up your budget. It will just depend on your situation, and what you prefer/can do. Either way, I've found that the venue and catering are going to be the biggest costs for your wedding day, so be prepared for that.

TIP: For your overall budget—if it is possible for you—add a bit of money on top, just to give you a buffer. This could be anywhere from rounding budgets to the nearest ten, to adding a few thousand on top of the overall amount. This can give you a little trick of the mind; it will feel better to over-budget and come under, than to under-budget and go over! Do be careful, though, if you think this won't work for you; some people will see the buffer as just more room for more. But I know that for us this worked well, and it may also suit you.

YOUR STORY BUILDING BLOCK #34: HOW MUCH YOU WILL BE SPENDING ON YOUR WEDDING DAY

How much do you want to spend on your wedding day?
How much CAN you spend on your wedding day?
What is your budget for each of the smaller items?
What is the total sum of these smaller item budgets?
What research do you need to do?
What is your absolute maximum budget?
What other expenses are going on in your non-wedding life that you can foresee (new house, baby on the way, etc.)?
How will this affect how much money you can spend on your wedding?
How much is anyone else contributing (parents, bridal party, etc.)?
Who do you need to have a conversation with?
When will you need to have these conversations by?

How much are the bridal party contributing?

As mentioned earlier, in our families, our parents pay for the bridal party. My parents paid for all the bridesmaids' dresses, shoes, jewellery and clutches, and Luke's parents paid for all of the groomsmen's suit hire, shoes, socks and other accessories. Our parents paid equally for our 2 flower girls' dresses, shoes and accessories.

This may or may not be what you choose too. Other options are to have the bridal party pay for their own attire. For my bridesmaids, they all had the same style and colour dress. For other weddings, I know of bridesmaids who were given a colour but were able to choose the dress style, particularly because they were paying for their own dresses. This way they could choose something they liked and that suited them, supposedly with the intention of being able to wear the dress again (contrary to popular belief, I've never actually met someone who has worn a bridesmaid dress again). Alternatively, you can go halves in the outfits, or ask your bridal party to contribute a certain amount. There are all sorts of options and combinations of how you can do this. If you are considering asking the bridal party to contribute, then how much they can afford might come into play.

Maybe what your bridal party contributes to are the extra events for your wedding: the Buck's night/stag do and the Bridal Shower/Hen's night kind of events. Other than agreeing on a date, these events were totally left to our bridal party. Luke and I didn't know any real details of these events until we rocked up to them. The bridal party organised and paid for everything for these events: the invites, the catering, the games and any other forms of entertainment. With paying came the responsibility and the control over these parties, which were another thing off our plates, so we were happy.

YOUR STORY BUILDING BLOCK #35: HOW MUCH YOUR BRIDAL PARTY IS CONTRIBUTING

What are the payment options available for how your bridal party could contribute to your wedding?

How much, if at all, do you want your bridal party to contribute to your wedding costs?

If you do wish them to contribute:

What happens if one or more are unwilling to contribute?

What happens if one or more are not able to contribute?

What happens if one or more are delaying payment and are not cooperating?

How will you feel if costs fall on you?

How will you keep things equal and fair between all bridal party members?

How will you communicate these decisions with your bridal party?

How will you manage payments?

This is the big question. This is going to make or break your budget, as how you manage your payments will show how in control of your wedding budget you are. Managing your budget will mean knowing what needs to be paid and by when, how much is going out (and maybe coming in) and being able to communicate this successfully with anyone else who needs to know.

Depending on what you prefer, having one person manage the budget might be a lot more convenient than having 2 or more people. If one person is particularly good at managing money or being organised, you may find it is easier for only that person to keep track of all the costs by a means they prefer, so that nothing is accidentally forgotten or paid twice. For us, after our parents opened the conversations with our wedding suppliers and vendors whilst I was in New Zealand, I took over when I got back and was the sole money manager. Because I am the

Organising Queen, this role suited me. I managed all the budget in a way that made sense to me, and then also communicated everything with the parents in an efficient way. If I was managing the budget with someone else, be it someone living with me or in another house, unless we were always together when working on the budget, one person would be more up to date than the other, and miscommunications and misunderstandings could pop up. Whenever I've worked on something like this with a family member or friend, I've always found one person ends up being the one who *knows* the detail better than the others, because they either created the managing document, or it's on their computer, etc. So, you may also find that one person managing the budget, whilst a relatively decent-sized job, will be a smarter choice.

I have already introduced to you in chapter Practical Bits the super Microsoft Excel spreadsheet that helped me keep track of all the money for our wedding. Spreadsheets are designed for the management of all sorts of numbers, so take advantage of them.

I used my wedding budget spreadsheet to keep track of:

1. All of our wedding items
2. The amount we budgeted for each item
3. The final quote for each item
4. When different instalments were due
5. The amount we had already paid towards each item (for example, deposits paid, etc.)
6. What payments each side of the family was responsible for
7. Total costs

A spreadsheet is basically a giant table with columns and rows. Each numbered point above was a different column title in the spreadsheet, and each wedding item ran down the left side, so that each item had its own row. The trick was to keep updating the spreadsheet and keep on top of it. As long as this was done regularly, it was really easy to manage. This spreadsheet was kept simple and clear, and this made it easier to update. I made sure that, as soon as we had a new quote or had made a payment, I would open my laptop and update my spreadsheet within 24 hours. I was on my laptop a lot these days, so this was an easy convenience. Just a couple of clicks away. To make this step even easier, I had my spreadsheet just sitting on my desktop, so it was there staring me in the face as soon as I opened my laptop, and I didn't have to click through lots of folders before getting to the spreadsheet. Making life easier 101 TIP: Make the task as easy as possible in order to maintain it[2]. More information on the wedding budget template can be found in the Bonus Material section of this chapter.

What tools do you have at your disposal to help you track your wedding bill?

As well as the tracking, there will be a lot of communicating with others to make payments, whether your parents are contributing to your wedding payments or if it is just you and your partner. This also includes communicating with the wedding vendors and suppliers, i.e., the payees. At first it can be very uncomfortable asking anyone, let alone parents and possibly in-laws, "Can you please pay this amount into this account for these items by this

---

[2] Check out Chapter 6: 'Motivation is Overrated: Environment Often Matters More', p81-90 in James Clear's book *Atomic Habits* for more on designing your environment to suit your habits (2018, Penguin Random House, UK).

date?". You might have no problem doing so, but it is also completely normal to feel uncomfortable about discussing budget and money related things. As discussed in depth in the <u>Communication</u> chapter, the key I found was to be clear about what the cost was for, but also, give plenty of notice when a payment is coming up. This will help manage everyone's expectations, and reduce the number of surprise costs, so that those that genuinely come up unexpectedly, are acceptable. If you spring all wedding payments upon a payer as last minute surprise costs, they may start to get frustrated with you. Give a heads up where you can, and multiple ones as well. After all, it's not only yourself who can be uncomfortable when it comes to money. So, give plenty of notice so payers, whoever they are, can get comfortable with and prepare for the upcoming costs, especially the big lumps you will be dealing with for your wedding. The more transparent you are with the payments people need to make, the better they'll be received. Whether the person who is managing the money and the person/people who are paying for the wedding are different people or not, clear communication will be really important and relevant to ensure payments are paid on time.

YOUR STORY BUILDING BLOCK #36.A: HOW YOU WILL MANAGE YOUR MONEY

How will you want to manage your wedding payments?
What money management tool will you like to use for managing your wedding budget?
What money management methods have worked well in the past?
How many people would you like to manage your wedding budget?

Who would be great in this role?

When can you speak to this person/these people?

How comfortable do you feel about having conversations about money?

What could you do to ease any uncomfortable feelings?

When someone else other than yourself is paying for your wedding—usually parents—it can be tricky to navigate. Everyone has different styles of managing their own money, and everyone has different styles of making payments. Some people put things off until the last minute, some people negotiate as much as possible, and others will pay promptly to get the task out of their hair. For our wedding, both pairs of parents were really proactive when making payments. They took on a pay-as-you-go approach for everything; i.e. as costs came up, they were happy to pay them promptly. For some of the bigger items, such as the venue and the wedding dress, we did not need to pay them all in one go; we could pay in instalments. TIP: If given the choice, opt for payment in instalments. This will help minimise financial pressure wherever possible, and spread out the spending.

Working with our parents was a blessing. We were all on the same page from the beginning with regards to expectations, and that made the entire process smooth sailing. Even though I was the only one really managing the money, I still kept everyone involved and communicated all costs. I kept my spreadsheet organised and up to date, so that if anyone asked me a money-related question, I could derive the answer by quickly checking my spreadsheet, and getting back to them promptly. TIP: For anyone who is in a similar situation, send out a spreadsheet to your wedding payers via email regularly so that everyone can look through it at their own pace. Make it as easy as possible for everyone to work with you, so that your wedding payers feel at their most comfortable with your money management. Maybe you don't want particular payers to see the full budget, and that is fine. This might still be a useful tip for just between you and your partner.

What made the difference in Luke's and my families was that they held similar values and worked alongside each other very well. This is partly due to the fact that our families had been acquainted for a good 4 years already before we got married, so they felt secure and trusted each other. When families do not know each other well enough, come from different backgrounds or cultures, language barriers are present, or they simply do not like or trust each other, something like splitting wedding costs between the families becomes a big issue, and needs to be handled with care. This is when discussing how money will be managed becomes quite an important discussion from the onset. I have seen first-hand how different ways of paying can impact on families, where the parents have paid for the wedding. There have been several weddings where one side of the family bore all the costs and expenses, and the other half of the family only paid back their half of the final wedding bill after the actual wedding. This can put a lot of financial pressure on one side of the family, and can create tension before the families have even become one. Some cultures believe only the family of one half of the couple needs to pay for a wedding, but if the couple aren't both from that culture, this can create issues. Subsequently the couples I know who have been in this situation haven't got great relationships between their parent-in-laws. Not necessarily bad, but not great. Sometimes you and your partner have to act as the middle people for communications, and this can be hard.

> *How will the person/people managing the payments communicate between themselves and others?*
> *What are your main concerns when it comes to managing payments?*
> *What similarities/differences exist between the way you and your partner handle money and payments?*
> *What similarities/differences exist between the way your family and your partner's family handle money and payments?*
> *Where are your weaknesses in your money communications?*
> *Who could you talk to, to get advice on communicating with certain people/family members?*
> *What options do you have with your family?*
> *Who do you need to inform regularly about the status of your wedding payments?*
> *How will you regularly update the status of your wedding payments?*
> *When will you set aside time to devote to money management?*
> *What will happen if your money management plan does not work?*
> *Who can you ask to help you keep on top of your wedding money management?*
> *How can you remind yourself?*

How can you bring costs down?

Weddings aren't cheap. In general, most people, even if they have plenty of money to spend, will try and find ways to be money savvy when spending. Your wedding is no different. In the consumer world out there, anything with the word 'bridal' attached to it apparently gets a green light to increase the price, so cutting costs wherever you can will be important.

You can get super creative with how you're going to save some money. Below is a shortlist of some—not all—ways in which you can bring costs down:

- Negotiate discounts
- Buy on sale
- Make it yourself
- Borrow items
- Bulk buy
- Utilise your connections and see who knows who to get mates' rates
- Shop at non-bridal shops
- Be flexible with the 'extras' you can pay for
- Ask yourselves what you really want or need and if it is really worth it
- Money-back bonds and post-wedding options with vendors and suppliers

What other ways can you think of to bring costs down?

Some of the options above will be a trade-off between time and money. For example, making items yourself. I initially wanted to make my own bouquets out of fabric. When it finally came time to decide which way I would go with the bouquets, I realised I would have to make 5 bouquets, and making them was going to be very time-consuming. I decided that my time was going to be better utilised elsewhere—I was busy enough as it is—so we decided to go with fresh flowers. But for other items, the trade-off of time for money was worth it. We had fun making a few items for our engagement party. We had some decorative birdcages left over from my 18th birthday party that we re-used for our table centrepiece decorations. I spray painted them and added some candles, and these were perfect with a couple of fake flowers we had lying around too (TIP: Re-use any decorations you've used for previous parties. These tend to get shoved in spare rooms or sheds, but give them a new lease of life and re-use them for small wedding bits). I also saw on Pinterest an idea for how our name placements could be for our engagement party, and wanted to see if my dad and I could make them. We would have to cut a 1-inch thick log into 1-inch lengths, cut a little slit into the flat of one side and voilà—a name placement holder. My dad almost broke his thumb, but he managed to cut these for us while I varnished them and created the name placement cards. All these items we had lying around in the garage or in the backyard garden—free! TIP: Pinterest can be your best friend during your wedding planning months. I got so many amazing and beautiful wedding ideas, but also creative and cheap ideas as well.

For the wedding day, we decided to carry on the bird cage theme. We bought 2 mini birdcages that could hold each of our wedding rings, and the flower girls could hold a birdcage each. I sewed a couple of tiny cushions to go inside them with ribbons, all from scraps I had around the house, and ta-da, we had our ring holders. There were several other items that we did ourselves, and were able to reduce our costs. For example, if it was cheaper to print something ourselves, then we would do so. We had fancy acrylic invitations, but we also had a small paper note that slid inside the invitation envelope. This was going to be cheaper to print ourselves on some nice paper, rather than get the company who created our main invitation to print it. We also sealed and posted the invitations ourselves, otherwise this was another additional cost. Basically, every task was an additional cost, so wherever it was possible for us to do it ourselves, we did. And with the invitations, wherever possible, we gave invitations in person instead of by mail, saving on postage costs. Do as much as you can yourself, wherever the time-money trade-off is worth it!

YOUR STORY BUILDING BLOCK #37: GETTING CREATIVE ON SAVING MONEY

What could you use that is lying around your house/your parents' house/your friend's house for your wedding?

What items are worth the trade-off of time for a reduction in costs?

What would you like to make for your wedding?

What can you do for your invitations to save money?

Which guests could you give invitations to in person instead of by post?

How much money are you saving by doing these actions you've come up with? Ensure your money management tool reflects this!

While we did look at bridal and formalwear shops for my bridesmaids' dresses, we got lucky and found them off the rack at a non-wedding shop, no alterations needed, and they had pockets! If you can find your wedding items at non-wedding shops, you are almost always going to find they are cheaper. The shop we ended up buying the bridesmaids' dresses from was the equivalent of a modern women's fashion brand shop along the high street. The dresses were very formal looking, but were a third of the price of the average bridesmaid dress at a specialised bridal shop. They also didn't need to be shortened or altered in any way. TIP: The part of the bridesmaids' dresses that had the biggest influence on whether we required alterations or not was the dress length. My bridesmaids' dresses were calf-length, so none of them needed alterations. If the dresses were to the floor dresses, they definitely would have needed hemming as most dresses are made longer than required for mass production. So, if you wish to cut costs or avoid extra tasks, consider the dress length for this. It will just then be a matter of ordering the correct sizes. The shop we bought the dresses from also offered free delivery to our door. This just went to show that you do not need to limit yourself to only bridal shops; you can find things elsewhere too and they are almost always going to be cheaper. It's just a matter of looking around and doing a bit of searching (again, a time-money trade-off).

For the bigger items, such as photographers, florists, etc., shop around and get at least 3 quotes. The example mentioned earlier was our florist. We had no idea on how much a florist would be. We visited 4 places; 2 were around the same price, one was double the price of the first 2, and the 4th was half the price of the first two. We ruled out the super expensive one because for the same quality of flowers it was way too expensive. If we had only visited the most expensive florist, we would have accepted that price without knowing any different. We were able to cut our florist bill in half only because we had shopped around. So, do shop around, and this will give you a little bit of an indication of what the average prices are for what you want, for that particular industry, in your area. Any wedding statistics—such as the reports in the Further Reading section of this chapter—will also help give you an industry standard.

Similar to the invitations, there are a lot of 'extras' you can have for your wedding venue, your wedding dress, etc. All these extras are likely to be additional costs. Be ruthless with your extras if you need to be. Luke and I made some to-the-point decisions on what extras we could cut from the wedding. Particularly for the reception venue, there are usually a lot of extras you can choose from: fancy lighting, fabric from the ceiling, sashes on the chairs, etc. Initially we wanted to hire gold cutlery and charger plates for our table settings, just because gold went with the theme. It turned out to be something like $12AUD per charger plate to hire. I can't remember what the total charge was for gold cutlery as well, but we had 220 guests. If we could *just* bring it upon ourselves to be happy with boring old standard silver (please read that in a sarcastic tone), we would get the cutlery for free as this was the option that was included in our package. Either way, whether the cutlery was gold or silver, the guests would be eating just fine. We decided that this was a cost we could live without, as it was not worth an extra $500AUD and more. By being flexible in a few areas and really thinking about how much a particular 'extra' would impact the experience of you or your guests, you will be able to cut a few costs on the 'extras' side of things. Opt for the options that are included in your wedding packages, as opposed to paying for the fancier options, if you don't feel they are worth the extra cost. If you do warrant it worth the cost, then by all means that is fine too!

YOUR STORY BUILDING BLOCK #38: THE COST OF 'EXTRAS'

What wedding items do you consider non-negotiable?
What wedding items are you more flexible on?
On a scale from 1 to 10, with 10 being 'I really want it' and 1 being 'I don't want it at all', how much do you want [this item]?

On a scale from 1 to 10, with 10 being 'I really need it'
and 1 being 'I don't need it at all', how much do you
need [this item]?
How realistic is [this item] in your wedding?
How will [this item] improve your wedding, and the
whole wedding experience?

Another thing to really utilise is your connections. Especially if you are local to the area, or if you know people in wedding industries. These connections can help you get information, insider knowledge and tips, but also discounts on services. And again, get creative with the 'services'; you can totally stretch what this means, as I'm not just talking the traditional wedding services. For us, here are some of the connections we utilised: our wedding car was provided by a family friend for free; Luke was gifted a keg of beer for his Buck's night, cutting beverage costs; we were able to buy wedding rings at wholesale prices, for my engagement ring and both of our wedding bands, from a long-time family friend who was a jewellery-maker; and we were able to swing a few things to enjoy a decent coffee machine and barista at our reception (we are Italian—a good coffee is a must!). I also found a couple of string instrumentalists through musician friends who charged smaller rates than the better-established bridal quartets out there, and they performed just as beautifully.

In terms of the more traditional forms of wedding services where you can utilise your connections, one big example I can give you is our church. One half of my family have been attending our local church for over 50 years and are well-known in the community. It made sense to get married at this church above the others for sentimental reasons alone, but the fact we were part of the local parish was unintentionally in our favour as it helped to reduce the costs for the ceremony. Other couples who were not part of the local parish had an additional (and not small) cost if they wanted their wedding at this particular church. This may be something you wish to consider for your own religion or any other connections you have for your ceremony location.

YOUR STORY BUILDING BLOCK #39: CONNECTIONS

What connections do you have that you could utilise?
What connections do you have that you WANT to utilise?
Who do you know who might have a connection they would be happy to negotiate a service from?
Who do you know who can help you out with particular wedding items?
When can you talk to these people?
Which wedding vendors that you've already hired might have connections and deals going with other vendors, who you might be able to receive a discount from?
What LOCAL connections do you have that you could utilise?

One of the other options listed to help reduce costs is to buy some things in bulk. The more business you give a company, the more likely you are going to get a discount. This applies particularly if you have a large guest list or a larger number in your bridal party. I found this useful for party favours and invitations, and when you have 3 or more bridesmaids, most hair and make-up artists offered bulk prices. We also negotiated a lot with our wedding venue. Because we got married at a hotel, our immediate family stayed overnight and we had a catered breakfast the morning after the wedding. So not only were we organising a sit-down meal wedding reception for 200+ guests with them, but we also organised around 10 hotel rooms for the night and breakfast for 40 people the next day. This was more than the average business they get, so this provided us with a bit more negotiating power.

An accidental way to get costs down was to speak up when things went wrong or if any poor service was received. Now, I don't mean to be a pain in the backside and constantly complain to the companies you're working with just for the sake of a discount; I'm definitely not advocating to be one of those people, and I certainly am not one myself. But if a genuine reason comes up, don't hesitate to ask for a discount, a replacement, or some form of compensation. For example, our invitations had a printing issue for a large portion of the invites. When I approached the business provider, they offered us 2 options: to replace the misprinted ones or get a 50% discount. After speaking to our parents and Luke, we opted for the discount. We had acrylic laser-printed invitations and to just throw away half of them seemed excessively unnecessary. While there was a printing issue, it was not hugely noticeable and weighing up our options, it was not worth throwing them away. So, we chose the discount. This saved us 50% on an originally expensive invite. We also had an issue with our party favours, as some of them broke in transit. We were offered the same recuperation, and this time we opted for the free replacement. The broken party favours were rendered totally useless, so the refund was not worth not giving some guests a party favour, therefore we chose the replacement.

The point is that, if something goes wrong, don't be afraid to speak up. All of the vendors and suppliers I worked with (except my rogue one) actually treated our wedding quite sensitively. A lot of them were small businesses, and I found they were very keen to provide a near-perfect experience. I felt their investment in the wedding too, so as soon as we received a service that was less than promised, they were happy to fix it. They really were easy to work with. Word of mouth is something businesses rely on as a main source of advertising, especially small and self-employed businesses, and therefore they generally wish to ensure they provide great customer service. But, again, don't try and take advantage of this!

What can be particularly tricky is if you're working with a family member or a friend for a wedding service. It can be hard to speak up about any unexpected results or errors without thinking you'll offend them and damage the relationship. Judge this decision as you see fit. If it's worth being honest, the feedback could actually benefit them in the long run; they're a business owner at the end of the day and assumedly would care about their service too. But, if you are happy to cut them some slack, or if it's not a big deal to you, then maybe you choose to not say anything. It depends who it is and what the relationship is like.

If you do choose to notify them about something you're not happy with, think about the best way to approach it with that person. Instead of pointing out a problem, maybe suggest the solution, so it sounds like an alternative instead of a rejection. Maybe you throw in a compliment of another part of the service, or maybe you go the totally transparent route and tell them you feel bad or guilty about what you're doing. It can be hard, but think of the alternative—**what might happen if you don't speak up?** Maybe they'll expect you to come back to them for future services because they thought you were happy with it. Maybe they go on treating customers as they've done you. You may start a domino effect here. Whatever that answer is, it might be enough to motivate you to speak up.

YOUR STORY BUILDING BLOCK #40: DAMAGED GOODS, MISTAKES AND ERRORS

How do you feel about speaking up on any less-than-promised services you receive?

How can you approach these businesses in a professional manner?

How can you use this opportunity to develop your confidence?

The last area to mention is to get some money back. These are all the last little bits that generally happen post-wedding, but because of that, they can be forgotten.

Some of the side-equipment given to us for our wedding—florist buckets and boxes, for example—we found that, in the fine print of our contract, if returned, would warrant a small money-back. This is a detail that could easily have been left behind and forgotten, but gave us an extra couple of hundred dollars back on the wedding costs. Every bit counts, so check out your contracts and even ask questions to see if this might apply with your wedding vendors. There is also the option to sell some of the items you bought for your wedding after the event is all said and done. More on these options in the Post-Wedding chapter, but keep this in mind to help recoup some, if only a little part of, the wedding expenses.

YOUR STORY BUILDING BLOCK #41: MONEY-BACK OPTIONS

What bonds or money-back options have been given to you?

What wedding items could you sell post-wedding?

In what other ways could you recoup some of the wedding costs?

Suggestion Box

1. KEEP YOUR PAYMENT DEADLINES IN ONE PLACE.

There is such a huge part of money management that comes down to keeping organised. This ties in really closely with chapter <u>Practical Bits</u> earlier, so you may wish to revisit that chapter. As you commit to suppliers and they give you deadlines for payments, collect them and put all your payment information in one place. This will need to include when a payment is due, how much of a payment you have already paid, and when the payment is complete. A diary or a digital reminder system will help a lot here.

2. USE MICROSOFT EXCEL OR ANOTHER MONEY MANAGEMENT TOOL.

I highly recommend tools such as Microsoft Excel to track your money, as this is exactly what they are made for: dealing with numbers. This way you won't have to do any of the adding up yourself. There are many YouTube videos and online tutorials to give you a crash course on how to use a spreadsheet. But if you want to save yourself some time, you can check out the spreadsheet I used myself in the Bonus Material section to help you track your wedding bill.

3. KEEP IT NEAT, CLEAR AND SIMPLE.

You are going to want your wedding money management system to be as approachable and easy to deal with as possible. When things are messy or complicated, you have to make sense of it all first *before* you can actually deal with the problem. That is when you're most likely to ditch the task and put it off, because there is an extra step of understanding it first. This usually ends up with the task growing and becoming even worse to deal with. However, if you choose to track your wedding bill, keep it neat and 'pretty looking'. Write in neat handwriting, or use clear and legible digital means. If you make a mistake, or have lines going everywhere, clean it up. PLAN how you want to present it first, and then set things up. If you start without a plan, half way in you're more likely to have additional ideas of what to include, which mess up what you have created so far. The clearer, simpler, and 'prettier' your money tracker is, the more attractive it will be to you, the happier you will be working on it, and the easier it will be to work with.

4. KEEP IT UP TO DATE.

Similar to the previous point, if you let your money tracker go and do not update it regularly, then the task to update grows and it becomes too big and daunting. If you can do a little bit of work regularly and keep on top of it, this will not happen. You can peel one carrot a day for 7 days, or you can peel 7 carrots in one day. Both ways you will get 7 peeled carrots, but one carrot a day is a smaller job and more approachable (weird analogy but you get the point!). My way of doing it was, as soon as I had a piece of information to insert into my money tracker, I would make sure I updated it within 24 hours. This little rule I gave myself ensured the information was fresh in my head and my tracker was constantly up to date with minimal work.

5. GET SEVERAL QUOTES FOR ALL THE MAJOR MARKING POSTS.

We got at least 3 quotes for each of our bigger wedding items, and found that they sometimes varied GREATLY. It was easy to see the more reasonable price points for an item when we had at least 3 quotes, so I recommend this, which will help to ensure you are not over-paying for something.

6. DO SOME RESEARCH.

To help budget for your wedding, as well as getting several quotes, you can do some research to see what average costs are for different items. Check out wedding statistic reports for your country for the most recent year simply by Google searching them. For Australia and the UK, I have referenced 2 reports in this book for 2018 and 2017 respectively, which show the different wedding statistics and are really easy to read. I have included links to these in the Further Reading section, however these are current only at the time of writing —do a quick check for more recent ones.

7. HAVE A METHOD FOR MAKING HARD DECISIONS.

If you have a strict budget to stick to, you are probably going to have to make some emotional decisions on where to cut costs. For us, it was the difference between gold and silver cutlery. Was this really going to make a huge difference? We decided no, but you may have chosen yes, which is fine. When it comes to decision making, it is important to have a back-up plan to help you make your decisions. One way could be the following method:

Ask yourself these 2 questions for any particular detail:

1. "How much do I want this?"
2. "How much do I need this?"

Rate your answer on a scale from 1 to 10, with 10 being 'I really do' and 1 being 'I don't at all'. Compare the answers, and then compare your answers to those of your partner. This just might be enough to help you make your final decision.

You may have a different idea on how to make those hard decisions —you could literally choose rock paper scissors or flipping a coin as a way to decide —but decide on a method with the relevant parties early on and use this for any of the harder decisions you just cannot agree on.

8. GET CREATIVE ON HOW YOU CAN SAVE MONEY.

Negotiate, hire, bulk buy, borrow, make it yourself, family connections, secondhand —there are lots of ways to bring costs down. Utilise every single option available to you. There are more options than I have stated in this book too, so sit down with a blank page and pen and get creative. Think of all the ways you might be able to cut costs. Put silly, illegal or immoral ways on your list too. While you (hopefully) will not choose these options, they will still help your creative juices flow with ideas, and writing down the options you will not choose may actually give you new and better (and legal) ideas.

9. EVERY PENNY COUNTS.

Paying for a wedding includes the thousands of dollars you will spend on the reception venue, right down to the 79 cents you paid for some ribbon. INCLUDE EVERYTHING. It is in the detail, where you spend a couple of dollars here, a few more there, and then all of a sudden, you are down one hundred and you have no idea where it all went. If you are tracking your costs, every single item needs to be recorded, including the little ones. And trust me, there are going to be a lot of little ones. Keep the receipts for this reason to help yourself out.

10. DON'T FORGET ANY POST-WEDDING COSTS OR GAINS.

This may or may not be something you want to include in your wedding budget but definitely needs to be something considered (more on this in the Post-Wedding chapter). You may damage hired goods and lose deposits; there's the cleaning fee of the wedding dress; any outstanding wedding payments that are due for completion post-wedding; etc. You may even wish to include some honeymoon costs in your wedding budget. But it's not only about the costs; there are also the opportunities to get money back. Any bonds that need claiming upon the return of goods; any damaged items or errors on the behalf of the company providing them (for example, a broken vase that may have been delivered on the day, rendering it useless and resulting in one table potentially not having a centrepiece).

Please do not take advantage of these businesses. In my experience they worked just as hard to make the day go beautifully for us as we did. But on the off chance something does go wrong, don't be afraid to chase it up.

Some of these points here you obviously cannot plan for, like the damaged goods. But for the ones you can, like cleaning fees for dresses and suits, don't forget to consider these and whether or not you'd like to include these in your wedding budget.

Summary of Questions in this Chapter

YOUR STORY BUILDING BLOCK #33: WHO IS PAYING AND HOW YOU WILL BE SPLITTING THE COSTS

Who will be contributing to your wedding costs?

How are costs being split between paying parties?

How are all parties agreeing on the matter?

How will they be paying, i.e. what's their approach (pay-as-you-go, lump sum at the end, cash, bank transfer, etc.)?

When will you receive the money to pay for items?

What will you do if you do not receive money as initially agreed?

Who needs to know about your answers to these questions?

How will you agree with the people involved in paying for your wedding (verbally, in writing, etc.)?

YOUR STORY BUILDING BLOCK #34: HOW MUCH YOU WILL BE SPENDING ON YOUR WEDDING DAY

How much do you want to spend on your wedding day?

How much CAN you spend on your wedding day?

What is your budget for each of the smaller items?

What is the total sum of these smaller item budgets?

What research do you need to do?

What is your absolute maximum budget?

What other expenses are going on in your non-wedding life that you can foresee (new house, baby on the way, etc.)?

How will this affect how much money you can spend on your wedding?

How much is anyone else contributing (parents, bridal party, etc.)?

Who do you need to have a conversation with?

When will you need to have these conversations by?

YOUR STORY BUILDING BLOCK #35: HOW MUCH YOUR BRIDAL PARTY IS CONTRIBUTING

What are the payment options available for how your bridal party could contribute to your wedding?

How much, if at all, do you want your bridal party to contribute to your wedding costs?

If you do wish them to contribute:

What happens if one or more are unwilling to contribute?

What happens if one or more are not able to contribute?

What happens if one or more are delaying payment and are not cooperating?

How will you feel if costs fall on you?

How will you keep things equal and fair between all bridal party members?

How will you communicate these decisions with your bridal party?

YOUR STORY BUILDING BLOCK #36.A: HOW YOU WILL MANAGE YOUR MONEY

How will you want to manage your wedding payments?

What money management tool will you like to use for managing your wedding budget?

What money management methods have worked well in the past?

How many people would you like to manage your wedding budget?

Who would be great in this role?

When can you speak to this person/these people?

How comfortable do you feel about having conversations about money?

What could you do to ease any uncomfortable feelings?

YOUR STORY BUILDING BLOCK #36.B: HOW YOU WILL MANAGE YOUR MONEY

How will the person/people managing the payments communicate between themselves and others?

What are your main concerns when it comes to managing payments?

What similarities/differences exist between the way you and your partner handle money and payments?

What similarities/differences exist between the way your family and your partner's family handle money and payments?

Where are your weaknesses in your money communications?

Who could you talk to, to get advice on communicating with certain people/family members?

What options do you have with your family?

Who do you need to inform regularly about the status of your wedding payments?

How will you regularly update the status of your wedding payments?

When will you set aside time to devote to money management?

What will happen if your money management plan does not work?

Who can you ask to help you keep on top of your wedding money management?

How can you remind yourself?

212

YOUR STORY BUILDING BLOCK #37: GETTING CREATIVE ON SAVING MONEY

What could you use that is lying around your house/your parents' house/your friend's house for your wedding?

What items are worth the trade-off of time for a reduction in costs?

What would you like to make for your wedding?

What can you do for your invitations to save money?

Which guests could you give invitations to in person instead of by post?

How much money are you saving by doing these actions you've come up with? Ensure your money management tool reflects this!

YOUR STORY BUILDING BLOCK #38: THE COST OF 'EXTRAS'

What wedding items do you consider non-negotiable?

What wedding items are you more flexible on?

On a scale from 1 to 10, with 10 being 'I really want it' and 1 being 'I don't want it at all', how much do you want [this item]?

On a scale from 1 to 10, with 10 being 'I really need it' and 1 being 'I don't need it at all', how much do you need [this item]?

How realistic is [this item] in your wedding?

How will [this item] improve your wedding, and the whole wedding experience?

YOUR STORY BUILDING BLOCK #39: CONNECTIONS

What connections do you have that you could utilise?

What connections do you have that you WANT to

utilise?

Who do you know who might have a connection they would be happy to negotiate a service from?

Who do you know who can help you out with particular wedding items?

When can you talk to these people?

Which wedding vendors that you've already hired might have connections and deals going with other vendors, who you might be able to receive a discount from?

What LOCAL connections do you have that you could utilise?

YOUR STORY BUILDING BLOCK #40: DAMAGED GOODS, MISTAKES AND ERRORS

How do you feel about speaking up on any less-than-promised services you receive?

How can you approach these businesses in a professional manner?

How can you use this opportunity to develop your confidence?

YOUR STORY BUILDING BLOCK #41: MONEY-BACK OPTIONS

What bonds or money-back options have been given to you?

What wedding items could you sell post-wedding?

In what other ways could you recoup some of the wedding costs?

Bonus Material

Wedding Budget Spreadsheet Template

This one is a bit too big to include here. Head to www.letsgetyourlifetogether.com/bridalcoaching to download this Microsoft Excel wedding budget spreadsheet template for free. Alternatively, you can customise the in-built budget template in Microsoft Excel.

Further Reading on Money

- **The UK Wedding Report 2018 by Bridebook.co.uk**

This report details statistics of the weddings of 3,000 UK couples who were married in 2017. Reports like this are super useful for setting up a budget and estimating how much different parts of your wedding might cost. You might like to find the latest one that is current at your time of reading.

- **Easy Weddings 2019 Australian Wedding Industry Report**

Same as the above report but for Australia. This report details statistics of the weddings of 4,100 Australian couples who were married in 2018.

These were easy to find, so have an internet search for your area (if it's neither the UK or Australia) and see what pops up.

Family Politics

So far throughout this book I have eluded to the fact that your wedding is probably going to be a collaborative effort between you, your partner, and/or your parents, other family members or friends. When we set out on our wedding planning journey, I really was not 100% expecting this. You may also be forgiven for thinking that your wedding is only about you and your partner, the couple in question. But for some of you, you'll probably learn very quickly, just as I did, that your wedding is completely a family affair. This somewhat makes sense, when you look at a wedding as a celebration of the marriage between two families. So be warned: things are about to potentially get real intimate with your fam bam.

Wherever there is a group of 2 or more people, there will always be differing opinions. Wherever there is a group of 2 or more people influencing a decision, compromising will be required. When this group of people are your family, interesting dynamics can unfold. It is these differing opinions and dynamics, and how you are going to handle them, that I call family politics.

Every family has its own politics. If we think about politics in general, we think of things like government, laws, and policies. When I talk about the politics of your family, I'm talking about your family's decision-making processes and the unwritten rules your family follows. The difference between your family and the government is that way more emotion is involved in your family, and this can make things a bit more delicate to deal with. Members of your government also typically change more frequently than members of your family; family you are stuck with, whether your family works well as a unit or not.

From talking to friends from other families, I've found that some family politics seem to be the same for a lot of families. For example, many families have an unwritten 'respect your elders' kind of rule, where you need to show respect to your parents, grandparents, aunties and uncles. This might be something you need to work with if older family members are involved in your wedding, especially if they have a strong voice. Other families have politics that are more unique to them, for example, a lot of your family politics might be tied up with your particular religion or culture.

And at the very individual level, you have the politics of working with different personality types. If you are like me and have parents involved heavily in your wedding planning process, this may or may not sit well with you. Even if this isn't your case, there can even be family politics just between you and your partner. Whichever it is, of all the events in your life, if there was ever a time where you were going to have to deal with family politics, your wedding is probably going to be it.

But first, a brain dump! Let all of your family frustrations go, in the space below. These can be personal, so if you don't want to use the space below, find a private space to unload—a journal, a digital file, etc.—where you know no one will find it by accident. We're not here to be cruel, but we all have frustrations, big and small. Sometimes just writing them down and getting them out can help the process of working through them. Not all frustrations we have need airing out (we can make informed decisions on whether or not it is worth addressing a family member), so this is why this brain dump requires privacy at first.

Your Story Brain Dump Space

My Story

Let me set the scene for this chapter with a little personal story. When I first saw *My Big Fat Greek Wedding* in 2002, I was in the cinemas with my mum, my dad, my brother, my nonno (grandpa), my nonna (grandma), my other nonno, my other nonna, and my aunty. If you have ever seen this movie, you might find this convoy of my family seeing this movie just as ironic as I did. Even at the tender age of 9, I knew that this movie was probably a little insight into what my own wedding was going to be like. It was not too far off.

The really basic story line of the movie is as follows: Toula was born into a Greek family in America, and was getting married to a non-Greek man, Ian. Her family is big, loud, and VERY involved in their wedding. They suck Ian right up into the family. The movie was mostly about Toula entertainingly struggling with the quirks of her family to say the least, but they got married and all was happy ever after in the end.

Change Greek to Italian, and change America to Australia, and you have my wedding. I come from a big, loud, Italian family. I am only a second-generation Australian, otherwise all my family is Italian. Anyone who has been to Adelaide or lives there knows that there are a lot of Italian-Australians there like me, and we all have stuck together with our cousins, our second cousins, probably even thirds. There are still members of my family that I still don't know how I am related to, but show up at all our family events. For some reason—and you can confirm this with my mum—I always knew I just wasn't going to marry another Italian-Australian. And I didn't. I brought home Luke, who was a blonde-haired blue-eyed tanned Aussie (I mean, technically he does have an Eastern European streak in him from his father's Yugoslavian side, but that's neither here nor there).

I can't tell you how accurate this movie was to my own dating experience. When Luke met my family, they loved him for one big reason: he loves his food. Anyone with a Mediterranean Nonna knows that, in general, if you bring home a partner who eats, she is going to like them. My Nonno also glows with delight at making 'the goat' for my husband; it is officially Luke's dish now. My grandparents were sold.

But even though, at the time of writing, my grandparents have had 7 years of knowing Luke, they still can't say his name right. With their strong Italian accent, Luke is forever 'Luca' to them. And Luke's mum, Jan, has always been 'jani' (sounds like 'Jenny'). It does not matter what we try, they just cannot say it properly. Fortunately, no one is offended by this, rather they all see it as quite hilarious, just like in the movie. And just like in the movie, when Luke met my family, he was completely overwhelmed. To this day, I am still teaching him the who's who of my family tree, and helping him get names right. The names are not too hard actually, because—just like in the movie—of the 200+ members of my family, there are about 8 male names and 9 female names that every member of my family shares. I kid you not—I counted. So, it is a safe bet Luke could probably guess someone's name and probably get it right.

I digress. The point I am trying to make is this, the movie is a pretty darn accurate representation of my family, so watch this to get an idea of just how much I know about a wedding being a family affair. To anyone else who's family is quite involved in their wedding—I understand.

As much as there are times when your family might frustrate you or times when you wish they'd back off, when you need them the most, they usually are the ones who drop anything to be there for you. Especially the big families—you're never short of people to find a helping hand!

YOUR STORY BUILDING BLOCK #42: FAMILY INVOLVEMENT

How involved is your family in your wedding?
How do you feel about that level of involvement?

If you have parents or family members paying for your wedding (or contributing to), this is where family politics can particularly start. Some parents really need to consider the reason they are paying for the wedding: is it to pay for their child's wedding or is it to *have a say* in their child's wedding? But regardless, the fact is how you feel about other people contributing to your wedding. As a daughter to parents who paid for my wedding, even if my parents were happy with handing the full buffet of wedding choices to me, I wouldn't have felt comfortable completely dictating how things were going to go. It was hard for Luke and I to not let both sets of our parents have a say in our wedding decisions, because it was their money at the end of the day. Luke and I were cool with this, but this meant that we did not always get exactly what we wanted. Not getting what we wanted was not *always* a bad thing either; for the majority of the situations for our wedding, it ended up just being the more considerate choice. Or, it was simply not something worth arguing over or ruining a relationship for.

However, even if you are paying fully for your own wedding, there will still be some family members who feel the need to have a say. Take these into consideration, but decide which ones are worth listening to. You can't please everyone, so don't even try to achieve this from the onset. But, if you have parents or other family or friends who actually do have some useful advice, or maybe even a small request ("Could you please invite so-and-so?"), try and get to a place of understanding with that person, see the reasons behind what they're saying, and you might find you actually do find it useful, especially if you haven't been married or in a wedding before. These people might have some advice based on experience. I'm probably going to say this more than once in this chapter, but weddings are just a moment in your life. Family relationships are going to be there after the wedding is long gone. Consider this fact when it comes to dealing with family politics.

One of the biggest things I find that a lot of people, including my family, have some family politics on, is the guest list, so let's start there.

The Guest List

Ah the guest list. Deciding who to invite and who not to invite. This can cause some real drama, because you have the potential to make some strategic passive-aggressive decisions here. All those weddings and events you have been excluded from in the past… now it's your turn.

Some of you might think I am being dramatic, but for others you know exactly what I am talking about. Half the time it's not even about being malicious; it's just some family tree branches have grown apart behind the scenes and your present or non-present invitation brings the issue front of stage. For some families, grudges ensue. For other families, it's a respect thing. Unless someone has done something to disrespect your family, then everyone gets an invite. Sounds very *The Godfather* I know, but the stronger your cultural and traditional heritage in your family, the more likely some unwritten respect rule exists like that. Oh, the drama that would ensue if you don't invite so-and-so.

My parents *insisted* on inviting some people, people that I had not even met. Who did not even come. Which we knew would not come, but we had to invite out of respect. I could not see the point in some of these invites, so, naturally, a few disagreements ensued. In the end, I figured it was not worth it, because ultimately it wasn't really negatively impacting Luke and I. For this situation the offense caused by not inviting someone was just not worth not printing out that extra invitation, especially when we knew they would decline anyway.

Despite not coming from a huge family, don't you worry, my husband's side of the family rose to the occasion and met us pretty equally for the number of guests, which was great; it meant my family wouldn't be swallowing up Luke's. This is how our guest list reached 250, and 220 of those RSVPed yes and attended our wedding.

Quick note on the topic of RSVPs: invitation politics. More specifically, the font. TIP: Ensure the font type and font size on your invitations is big and clear enough to be read easily. Our invitations were already off to a not great start on being easy to read, because they were clear acrylic invites and you needed to have the right background to actually read it. Because of this, we had to make sure that the cursive flowy wedding-style text was legible. The printing issue we had didn't help the matter. There was definitely a bit of fussing about this, and I genuinely don't know if anyone actually did have trouble reading our invites. I wouldn't be surprised if some of our older guests had trouble. Ours aside, I have seen some really poor font choices on wedding invitations, where you needed a degree in typography to work out the letters. This is down to good design, but you don't need to overthink it. Use this rule of thumb: If your grandparents can read it, then you're good to go.

Back to the guest list. Because our guest list was so large already, we decided to have an adults-only wedding, which is a controversial decision on its own. Family politics amber alert. I'm going to stay on this topic for a little bit. Our guest list was large enough for us; had we invited kids, if I recall correctly, it was going to add another 50 names to our guest list. Sorry, no. The cost just wasn't warranted.

Not everyone agrees with a 'no-kids' rule at weddings, so if you decide to also have an adults-only wedding, you may very well be informed by a few family members of their thoughts on the matter. Whether you chose to have an adults-only wedding for the same reason as we did, or for any other reason, that's your choice. If it's because your guest list is getting long, keep in mind too that, the larger your guest list, the more limited you may be with reception venue choices too, because not as many wedding venues hold the larger numbers. At 250 people, we had maxed out our choice reception venue, and simply could not have invited anymore people if we wanted to stay there.

YOUR STORY BUILDING BLOCK #43.A: GUEST LISTS
How will you decide on the size of your guest list?
Who else gets a say in your guest list?
How will you decide whether to invite kids or not?

Everyone has different opinions on this. When it comes to kids, there are many reasons for and against inviting them. Some possible reasons (not all) are shown in the table over the page.

For:	Against:
You see a wedding as a family event, and kids are part of the family, so they get an invite.	A wedding, in most cases, is a formal event. You might just like to celebrate your marriage with adults only and without crying babies or kids running around.
You felt left out when you were a kid and weren't invited to weddings, so you don't want to do the same to other kids in your family.	You have a budget and inviting kids is the difference between meeting that budget and going over.
You like kids.	You don't like kids.
You have good childhood memories of a wedding being a fun event to get dressed up, so want to give this opportunity to kids in your family.	You have bad childhood memories of going to weddings and being bored, and don't want to give this experience to other kids.
You like some kids but not others, but it is an all-or-none situation, so you go with all.	You like some kids but not others, but it is an all-or-none situation, so you go with none.

Kids are a controversial topic because, well, they are obviously personal to their parents, aren't they? When you don't invite someone's kids, of course it can be read as a personal attack. Their immediate reaction can be, "Well, what's wrong with my kids? Why can't they come?" This is completely natural and normal. Some mums in particular might be at breast-feeding stages with their bubs, and the no-kids invite might pose a little extra obstacle they need to organise arrangements for first. For

example, they may respond by:
- Asking the bride and groom if they can make an exception and bring their baby/child;
- Finding a babysitter;
- Pumping breast milk in preparation, if they don't mind it;
- Giving the baby formula that night, if it's an option;
- Sneaking out of the reception for a bit if it is close and convenient;
- Mum not attending the wedding;
- Mum and partner not attending;
- Complaining to other family members;
- Sharing their opinion on the issue with the wedding couple;
- Not giving the RSVP on time, making the wedding couple chase it up;
- Not spending as much on the wedding gift;
- Etc.

These are just potential responses; some of these might seem appropriate to you and some may not.

There may also be other reasons why parents aren't able to separate from their children, reasons that might not be any of your business. No one knows truly what goes on behind closed doors in families. All we can be is understanding and respectful of privacy.

On the flip side, some guests will be thrilled to hear you are having a no-kids wedding because they finally get a date night with their partner and get to celebrate without having to worry about their kids or needing to leave early.

At the end of the day, it is totally up to you on your choices for your wedding. I just want you to be prepared, that in my experience, some family members might not be shy about verbalising their feelings about your choices to you, either directly or indirectly. This is background noise that you don't need while you're planning your wedding, and you can respond in a multitude of ways. When someone did say something to us, we just chose to be honest: we had such a big wedding guest list already, and inviting kids was not feasible. If your reason is that you don't like kids, maybe be careful how 'honest' you actually are; ideally you don't want to offend. Maybe offence doesn't bother you. If this issue comes to a head for you, here's a shortlist of potential responses that you can judge as either appropriate or inappropriate, but, technically, all are still possible:

- You could ignore them;
- You could explain to them your reasoning;
- You could tell a harmless white lie;
- You could tell them it's none of their business;
- You could tell them it's not up to them;
- You could apologise;
- You could turn around and invite the kids;
- You could roll your eyes at them;
- You could un-invite them;
- Etc.

How else could you respond?

How you approach this really depends on how close and how big of an impact this family member is in your life. Some families are strife with gossip and you hear from Uncle so-and-so that the son-in-law of his cousin is upset about your decision, or some line like that, so you may even have to consider the impact on the family as a whole. If it is someone you see a lot, it is going to be important that you address the situation in a way that both parties walk away understanding and satisfied. I say satisfied because if they have verbalised their upset with you, chances are they will probably still be upset walking away, but at least walk away with an understanding of why you did or didn't do something, and are therefore satisfied to move on. Time will heal the issue at this point. If it is someone who you only see once a year if you're lucky, someone you're not particularly close with, or for some other reason you aren't bothered with what they think, then maybe it's not so important to you to address the issue or protect the relationship. It is totally up to you.

There may be other major issues with forming your guest list that I have not touched on. You might not experience the same issues I have mentioned here either. But I have no doubt it will take a while to compile your guest list, with a lot of consideration, re-thinking and finalising. Quick TIP here: If you have had other parties in your recent past—birthday parties, etc.—where you can recycle the guest lists for your wedding guest list, do so. This will give you a head start and more importantly a starting point that you can move forward with.

YOUR STORY BUILDING BLOCK #43.B: GUEST LISTS

What issues are you concerned about that may come up for you in regards to your guest list?

Which way do you think might be the best way to respond?

How comfortable would you be dealing with confrontation about your guest list?

How would you like to be treated if roles were reversed?

What would your [mother/father/other parental figure/role model] advise you to do?

How important is this confronting family member to you?

What are the impacts going to be on the relationship with this person post-wedding?

What if it is a child who admires you who is the one upset that they weren't invited to your wedding—how would you approach a child?

One last detail that can come up for your wedding guest list is ex-partners. If you or your partner are still friends with exes, or your families are family friends with your ex's family, it may raise a question mark whether to invite them or not. It depends on how close your families are as well. You might be cool with it; you might all still be friends and this might not be an issue for you. Or you might not be cool with it, and feel uncomfortable with your exes or your partner's exes amongst your wedding guests. Speak to your partner if you're in this situation, and you potentially might also need to speak to your parents if they're family friends and there's a bigger picture relationship to consider. You, or maybe someone else more appropriate, may even wish to speak to the family friends in question, and explain to them the situation. It generally is pretty obvious why they aren't invited if you choose not to, but because the impact may potentially be on the family and not just the ex, it could be a nice gesture just to ensure the family members aren't particularly involved, if this is a concern of yours.

YOUR STORY BUILDING BLOCK #44: EX-PARTNERS AT YOUR WEDDING
How will you approach any exes in your guest list?
What do you feel comfortable with?
How will parents/partners react to this decision?
What extra measures do you feel are necessary to take to keep family peace but ensure comfort at your wedding?

The Seating Arrangement

Let's now move smoothly from the guest list and into the seating arrangement. If you have a stand-up cocktail event for your wedding, you escaped a task and a half—well done.

The seating plan will depend on the number of guests you have and the table layouts. Your tables could be circle tables, long tables, benches, bales of hay... whatever they are, they will influence your seating plan. They will determine how many people can sit at that table, and therefore how you are going to group people for each table.

Points to consider when it comes to seating arrangements:

- Divorced couples who are both in attendance, potentially with partners. This might not be a family reunion you want your wedding to be remembered for;
- Particular family members who do not get along. Maybe you have a few family feuds that haven't been resolved, or some family members are renowned for angry fighting with each other when they are less than sober. Another family reunion to avoid;
- Keeping the groom's side of the family separate from the bride's side. Maybe they aren't so happy family just yet and it's really important that they are not mixed;
- If you do invite kids, you can choose to either have a kids table to make it more fun for them, or seat them with their parents;
- Maybe you also seat all the grandparents and older aunties and uncles together so that they can talk to each other instead of being bored and alone at the table when all their children are on the dance floor.

Something else that you might like to consider is the actual environment of your reception. For example, I know for our wedding, we needed to consider how close elderly people were to the music speakers. A good 30% of our guests were over 70 years of age; we couldn't have any blown hearing aids on our account. So, when we seated these guests, my parents wanted to make sure they weren't too close to the DJ's speakers. We also had a very hot and humid Australian summer wedding day. Air conditioning was something we needed, but again, we tried to avoid having the elderly sitting directly under them because, I know in my family, they usually get too cold a lot quicker than the younger ones. Sounds specific and detailed, but some of you might be able to relate. Maybe this particular example doesn't apply to you, but maybe you're having an outdoor wedding and the weather on the day will need to be considered. Maybe you'd like to consider giant fans because your wedding is in the middle of summer, or you need to ensure warmth and dryness if yours is a winter wedding. Maybe you'd like to supply blankets for all the older guests to supplement the weather. A slight tangent but still related, these environmental considerations can potentially have an impact on your seating plan too.

YOUR STORY BUILDING BLOCK #45. A: SEATING PLAN AND ENVIRONMENT CONSIDERATIONS

What might you need to consider for your seating plan that is unique to your wedding?
What factors are important for you?
How do you want to arrange your guests?
What environmental considerations do you need to consider for your wedding venue?
What additional wedding items do you need to organise for these environmental considerations?

Overall, if the guest list took you a while, the seating plan will take you longer. Treat your seating plan like a jigsaw puzzle. It will come together in the end, you just need to wiggle and force some of the pieces together. Depending on how you work best, you can literally treat the seating plan as exactly that: a jigsaw puzzle. If you are a creative visual person like me and like to physically see a layout of the seating plan, then print and cut out all of your guests' names, draw up the venue and start moving names onto tables. You will be able to see where everyone is, and it is very easy to swap names in and out. If that isn't your preferred style, maybe you're more of a person who loves lists, or someone who loves a spreadsheet. Crack open Excel and type away. Maybe you like to use a good old-fashioned pad and pencil. There is no right or wrong way to work on your seating plan; only the right way for you and your partner.

If you're not creating the seating plan on your own (which is highly likely), then, as with any group dynamics, politics will ensue. Different people will have different thoughts of how you could seat so-and-so, and how you could split a particular group of people. In general, it usually flows that those seated closest to the front of the seating layout (usually also closest to the bridal table) are those closest in relation to the couple—parents, grandparents, etc.—and then work your way back. Hopefully none of your guests read into where they were seated. We didn't have this problem at our wedding (not that I know of anyway), but I have been to weddings where this was another obvious passive-aggressive move. If you have seated people right at the back or in a position where they can't see—is this some kind of a statement? Are you being shady and did this intentionally to someone for a particular reason? This may be your style, this might not be, but nonetheless, food for thought! Ultimately you can't please everyone, but also, don't stress about all these issues

I've mentioned. Not all of these issues are going to be your issues; maybe not even any. Some families are mild and reasonable people, so all of this so far in this chapter might sound way too dramatic for you. But for some families this is the norm, so I hope you find solace in that you are not alone in your experience. Other brides and couples are out there and will go, are going and have gone through it all too.

YOUR STORY BUILDING BLOCK #45.B: SEATING PLAN AND ENVIRONMENT CONSIDERATIONS

How do you want to work out the seating arrangement? What method works best for you? Who else do you need to speak to when creating your seating plan?

Let's take a moment to breathe.

If this is all feeling overwhelming, it's because it's written all in one lump—and you're probably also reading it all in one lump and getting social information overload. You have my permission to put the book down, mull over it for a bit, then pick it up again when you're ready.

Wedding Speeches

The next thing where family politics comes up, is in the wedding speeches. Speeches are pretty common at weddings, but it's entirely up to you as to whether you actually have them or not.

If you do decide to have speeches at your wedding, you'll first need to work out who will be saying a speech. Traditionally it has been the men: the groom, the father of the bride, the father of the groom, the best man. But more and more often now, the women are taking part in the speeches. For our wedding we went with the traditional route, plus our flower girls said a few words. This was our choice; our mums were happy letting our dads do the speech on their behalf, and I was very happy leaving this task entirely up to Luke, as that would be one less thing I needed to do. As much as I would've loved to have stood with Luke and said a speech together, in a more progressive manner—and I have no problem doing a speech, so it wasn't nerves—I really could not bring myself to do any more for this wedding. I was reducing my responsibilities with that call, and I do not regret it because at the point of that decision I was very much ready to wave the wedding planning good-bye. So, the speech line-up was easy for us, but if you have step-parents and other figures who might be doing a speech at your wedding, you may need to give this an extra minute or two of thought.

YOUR STORY BUILDING BLOCK #46: WHO WILL BE GIVING YOUR WEDDING SPEECHES

Who will be giving speeches at your wedding?
What considerations need to be made in regards to your wedding speech line-up?
What order would you like the speech-givers to give their speeches?

Wedding speeches usually consist of pretty standard stuff: the thank yous to everyone for contributing to the day, complimenting of the newlywed couple and the bridal party, and thank yous to the parents for such a fine job they have done rearing the couple. Some throw in little stories and some humour. Of all the speeches I have heard—and there has certainly been a lot—most speeches follow along similar lines. As a result, that is what people have come to expect as a foundation to a speech. So, when you stray from that standard, or leave out a part, then you start to see side-eyes happening amongst the guests, and can maybe cause offense. Don't get me wrong—if a speech-giver wants to change up the game for wedding speeches and try something new, then straying from the standard can be a good thing. In my experience, these fresh speeches are due to a level of self-awareness on the speech-giver's behalf. But these aren't the speeches I'm talking about. I'm talking about *those* wedding speeches. The ones we see online. They are the giant elephant-in-the-room speeches, where everyone knows what is happening except the speech-giver. For example: I know of father's speeches where the mention of one of their children had been totally left out, but all the other children spoken of. Of families who don't get along, and the speeches REALLY reflecting that, to say the least. There has been many a drunken speech that just made you cringe listening to it again on the wedding video. Or the speech where the groom's Best Man demonstrates their closeness by describing the loss of the groom's virginity to a woman not the bride, or some other past story best kept private. And last but not least, the 'I'll just wing it on the night' speech. I have so far never seen this turn out well.

Oh, the family drama that can be instigated by a pot-stirring speech. Just google 'bad wedding speeches' to get the gist of how 5 little minutes can cause so much drama. Speaking of 5 minutes—watch out for the speech-givers that give books a run for their money. This is a speech etiquette that you will really want to remind your speech-givers of. Not for anything else, but when you have planned a speech timeslot in your wedding day's schedule that was not expected to be so long, you can hold up the whole reception, which can be inconsiderate to catering, the

DJ, photographer, and any other planned items on your wedding day itinerary. You don't want your wedding to be all about the speeches. But that's the thing: as the newlywed couple, the wedding speeches are typically not in your control. You don't directly get to decide what is said and for how long it is being said for. Most of the speech-givers have you included in their speech, so even if they were practicing their speech before the wedding, it is rarely going to be practiced on you or your partner. You simply have to have faith in your speech-givers.

What you can do is give your speech-givers some guidelines for their speech. From all the speeches I have heard in my life, I have compiled a list of points for good wedding speech etiquette:

Good Wedding Speech Etiquette

- Prepare and write the speech beforehand, or at least some dot points; don't wing it on the night.
- Get a trusted someone to listen and check your speech beforehand.
- Provide a maximum length of time the speech can go for. You might choose 10 minutes as an absolutely maximum or maybe even 5 minutes if you have a large number of speech-givers or have a tight schedule.
- If you are saying thank you notes, make sure you really have mentioned everyone, especially the obvious ones.
- No insults, especially towards any of the key players in the wedding.
- Keep as sober as needed until it is your speech time (depending on the person, a couple of drinks may actually help, just don't get too loose!).
- No embarrassing stories about exes of the wedding couple.
- Probably no 'losing your virginity' stories either.
- No airing out of any dirty laundry (check out the speech in the movie *27 Dresses* as an example).
- No hating on the in-laws.

YOUR STORY BUILDING BLOCK #47: WEDDING SPEECH ETIQUETTE

What kind of guidelines might you wish to give to your speech-givers?

Which wedding speeches have you heard and loved in the past?

Which wedding speeches have you heard in the past that you did not like?

How can you approach your speech-givers if you are concerned about their speeches?

If you are majorly concerned, who could you trust to listen to the speeches and ensure they're appropriate, without having to listen to them yourself?

Asking for Monetary Wedding Gifts

Wedding gifts, for my family at least, seem to be in a bit of a transition period. Traditionally, a couple would be setting up their first home together at the same time as they were getting married, so wedding gifts were physical gifts that helped them set up their home. But so many couples these days live in their own place prior to getting married, either individually or together, and already have a lot of their homewares. It is now more and more common to have a note included with the wedding invitation asking for monetary gifts as a wedding gift, but it still feels like it's in that in-between stage of whether or not it is appropriate. Is it rude to ask for money? For us, this decision was not without a bit of family politics. Asking for a monetary gift is becoming more common for weddings in our family, but there are still members who feel money is an impersonal gift. Luke and I wanted to include a note in our invitations for monetary gifts, not because we had a home already set up, but because we were moving to the other side of the world and money would be a greater gift in helping us set our home up in London. Considering these circumstances, we thought we could either leave it to chance, and guests may come to the same conclusion—that a monetary gift would be more helpful to us— or include a note asking for a monetary gift and potentially coming across as rude and offending some of the guests. We decided not to bother with this risk, and threw a note in the invitation envelope. We decided it was worth any rudeness we caused, because any gifts we received would have just gone into storage, potentially becoming obsolete or damaged, and that would just end up being a waste. If anyone said something, we would just be honest, and I believe our reasoning was fair enough.

If you *are* setting your house up at the same time as getting married and are open to wedding gifts, then a wedding gift registry is a way a lot of people approach it. This way, you can still choose the pieces you want to fit in with your own house and your style (after all, it is *your* home), and guests who want to give a physical gift can still do so. Maybe you are still happy asking for monetary gifts, knowing that you don't want all your homewares from the one place, which can be the downfall of a gift registry. Maybe none of this applies to you, and you'd still just prefer to ask for a monetary gift. This really depends on your preference and circumstances. Do what best suits you; there's no right or wrong answer here.

YOUR STORY BUILDING BLOCK #48: MONETARY GIFTS
What is the current state of your household set up, for you and your partner?

How do you feel about asking your guests for monetary gifts?

How big of an issue is this for your circumstances?

Who do you know who will get offended by being asked to give money?

How much does this person's opinion affect you?

Who is immediately involved in this decision (your partner, maybe parents, etc.)?

How do they feel about this?

Which way do you wish to ultimately go?

Bridal Party Politics

This chapter would not feel complete if I didn't mention your bridal party politics. I know personally and first-hand couples who have experienced some of the below hurdles with their bridal parties, so heads up guys.

Firstly, there is the choosing of your bridal party. The people in your bridal party are generally chosen because of how important they are in your life: close friends, siblings, other family members, etc. Choosing who is in your bridal party might be hard for you if you have more family and friends to choose from than bridal party spots to fill. You might feel you may offend some. If you feel like addressing the issue, you can remedy this by having a conversation with that person, explaining your choice and ensuring you haven't caused offence. I did this with one particular friend because I didn't want my choices to impact our friendship, and she was very understanding. Alternatively, there are other ways you can include those close friends and family, by giving them other roles in the wedding; maybe a marriage ceremony reading or something. Beyond this, if you've done all you can do and still have caused offence, then time will heal the situation at this point, if the relationship is meant to continue.

Once you have chosen, you might find your bridal party consists of a mixture of people who, in a lot of cases, don't necessarily mix in the same circles, and maybe don't even know each other prior to the wedding shenanigans. Maybe you have your partner's siblings in the mix, or family and friends who haven't met before. You just might find you have a collection of people on your hands who don't get along. That is hurdle number 1. Hurdle number 2 is you may not have the most proactive people, or ones who kind of fall off the radar and go missing all of a sudden when bridal party duties are calling. The bridal party are usually the ones who organise some of those extra wedding events, so if they have a track record of not being good at organising an event, it can definitely cause you concern and add to your plate of stress. Don't take this personally; it's not a sign they don't care as much about you. Organising events could just be a weak point for them, whether it was for you or for anyone else, including themselves.

Also, trying to get dates where all your bridal party can meet might be trickier than you think. Don't forget, they all have their lives going on in the background of your wedding too. They may not see your wedding as high a priority as you do. For our wedding, we also had a groomsman pull out a few months into our wedding planning period. When you ask people to be in your bridal party, you don't really consider anyone actually saying no. Luke and I weren't offended by this man pulling out of our wedding; in fact, we felt quite the opposite. We'd rather people who were up there with us to *want* to be up there with us, and if this wasn't the case then that was fine.

Whilst all these little political bridal party matters are

possible, and while I'm sure there are others out there that haven't been mentioned, they aren't necessarily going to happen to you. Great politics-free bridal parties do exist and you may have a fun and smooth sailing experience.

YOUR STORY BUILDING BLOCK #49: BRIDAL PARTY POLITICS

How well does your bridal party know each other?
How well does your bridal party work together?
Who are you most concerned about?
What can you do to improve your feelings about the bridal party?
How do you feel about getting involved in bridal party tasks in order for things to run smoothly?
How will your relationships be affected post-wedding?

General Family Politics

Family politics is related to decision-making, so it may come into every decision you make with regards to your wedding. So, I'm putting a general comment here that overarches everything. Family politics has the best chance of being resolved through communication, so this chapter pairs really nicely with the Communication chapter. As with all relations, communication is key to everything, and it plays a big role in dealing with family politics.

For every decision you make that impacts on your guests, you may wish to consider them in your decision-making process. You might like to answer questions such as the following:
- How can you ensure your guests are comfortable?
- How can you ensure they will have a good time?

- How can you ensure they will not get bored?

- How can you ensure they eat enough?

- Etc.

Our wedding was a family affair, and, as a family, we wanted everyone to have a good time. Before our wedding I was probably more ignorant to this than I thought. The wedding I had thought I wanted growing up was not the same as the wedding I ended up having. This is totally not a bad thing, because the wedding in my head was based only on what I wanted; the wedding that I got was what we all wanted, and that was even better. But as a result of that ignorance going in, I probably caused our parents more grief than necessary. I do also think on some decisions our parents caused me and Luke more grief than necessary too. That's just family for you. We go through life constantly growing and learning about our relationships with people. I do not for a second believe any family is free from disagreements. But sometimes, some things are just not worth your energy. For each decision you aren't agreeing on, someone has to decide whether it is worth getting what they want, over whatever the alternative is. Or you have to compromise. You physically and mentally cannot fight every single decision, because it is exhausting and not great for your health. So, choose your battles.

Wherever there are differing opinions there will be family politics. But at the end of the day, you cannot please everyone. REMEMBER THAT. Someone no doubt was not a fan of our wedding, and that is fine. All I can be sure of is that we didn't go out of our way to intentionally offend anyone, so if anyone *was* offended, it is really not our problem; it's theirs. Weddings are so easily judged, and some people will just try and look for something to complain about. Some people are just conditioned to look for the negatives. As long as you have been a good host and given an appropriate amount of consideration to your guests, then the rest is just based on the happiness and satisfaction of yourself and your partner, and to an extent your immediate circle of family and friends as well.

YOUR STORY BUILDING BLOCK #50: GUESTS AND GENERAL FAMILY POLITICS

How much consideration do you wish to give to your guests?

How important is it to you that your guests enjoy your wedding?

Where will be the limit to the extent of consideration you give to your guests?

What are your reasons for insisting on [this argument]?

What are your families' reasons for insisting on [this argument]?

How can you decide what will be worth insisting on, and what will not be?

What are the benefits/consequences of your decision post-wedding?

How will this impact your family relationships?

Suggestion Box

1. COMMUNICATE...

Family politics and family dramas can start when people start speculating, start gossiping with 'he said she said', or feel hurt. The best way I have found to sort this out is to communicate directly with people. Communicating and being honest will help everyone to move on. It is normally not knowing the reason behind an action that will cause feelings of animosity, so by communicating and showing understanding, it usually helps the situation a lot.

2. ...AND COMMUNICATE WELL.

You aren't only going to face external family politics; you may also find it will come up with your immediate circle when you make decisions for your wedding. On some decisions not everyone will agree, but what REALLY makes people stubborn and stand their ground is when your discussions become heated. Let's try and avoid that. You can only control your own communication skills, so when you communicate, it is important to stay in a level-headed state, use a tone that is not offensive or defensive, and to listen to what others have to say, making them feel heard. Revisit the <u>Communication</u> chapter for more on communicating skills.

3. BE OPEN TO COMPROMISE.

The wedding is not just about you. It is about you, your partner, and it can also be about your parents too. They've probably been dreaming of this day for longer than you have. No one's dreams are more important than another's, but remember that your dreams are very much from your perspective, and usually haven't considered others' perspectives. When you go into conversations about a decision, go in open to compromise. This may end up helping you get the outcome you want anyway, because when you are open, people around you will tend to feel obliged to be more open too.

4. YOU ARE ALLOWED TO AGREE TO DISAGREE, AND STILL COMPROMISE.

Just because you choose to do something, does not mean you necessarily agree with it. Personally, I would've preferred to have stood with my husband and said a wedding speech together. I think that is the more progressive way and that choice was available to me. But I was so done with the wedding planning, that I was happier for Luke to just take this role, and in doing so it took one thing off of my plate of things to-do. That was worth more to me than the fact that I didn't agree with it. That is an ok thing to do! You might want to do the reverse too: insist on doing something for the bigger stance it will have, even if you don't really want to. Maybe you want to stand and deliver a speech and go against the grain to be progressive, even though giving speeches terrifies you. Whatever it is, you can communicate that, whilst you do not agree with something, you are still willing to go ahead with it. This is a way to not compromise your own beliefs but still come to a resolution for a decision.

5. DECIDE WHAT IS WORTH FIGHTING FOR, AND WHAT IS NOT.

Continuing from the end of the last point, this doesn't mean giving up certain things you are passionate about. I know I definitely did not want only my dad walking me down the aisle; I wanted a more progressive option. You may have the power to have the overarching last say for your wedding day, but you will have to decide whether making yourself happy at the expense of the happiness of those around you is worth it. Some decisions can move into the 'too selfish' region too, especially if you do a hard-bargain for EVERY decision. Have some give and take room, decide which decisions are worth fighting for more than others. This way you won't lose yourself entirely in the wedding planning process, but can still keep the process a happy one for all involved.

6. CREATE SOME SPEECH GUIDELINES.

Please, please, please, create some speech guidelines to give to your speech-givers. You can use some of the points written earlier in this chapter, or you can create your own. You might need to speak to your caterer and find out how much time you have to play with when it comes to speeches, as there's normally a set amount of time between courses. You may trust your speech-givers and not need to worry about this, but if you just want to be sure, some wedding speech guidelines can give you some peace of mind.

7. REMEMBER, THE WEDDING IS FOR ONE DAY; THE FAMILY IS FOREVER.

Some weddings make or break family relationships. Unless you are happy to end a relationship, this is not something we typically want, especially if they are people you see a lot or are close to —parents, in-laws, maybe even your partner. Keep this in mind when you are making decisions, or when discussions become heated. You want to be able to come to a resolution that does not damage the relationship, because the relationship will usually be there long after the wedding day.

8. SOMETIMES YOU NEED TO FOCUS AND IGNORE.

Sometimes you just need to ignore the drama. You have enough drama going on with your wedding planning that you don't need to deal with anyone who is not a key player. Some people feel the need to share their opinion, even if it is not asked for or important to you. Some people just like to stir the pot. Some family members may even get jealous of you being in the limelight. All these actions usually say more about that person than you, so it's usually nothing personal, even if it does hurt. Beyond the people who are key players in your wedding, sometimes the best option is to ignore the noise and just focus on who and what matters the most.

9. YOU CAN'T PLEASE EVERYONE, SO DON'T TRY TO DO THE IMPOSSIBLE.

If you are a people pleaser, this may be a tough pill to swallow. You just aren't going to be able to please everyone at your wedding. We had 220 guests; we worried about them as a whole, and in sub-groups like the elderly, but we did not worry about what each individual would think, because there is no way all 220 people agreed on every detail in our wedding. Even just our immediate circle of important people —Luke, myself, our parents, grandparents —I am sure someone was not pleased with some detail or another. That is ok. Expect this and you simply won't be able to be disappointed.

10. KEEP IN MIND THE BIGGER PICTURE.

I realised very quickly that our wedding day was not just for Luke and I. It was for my parents, for Luke's parents, for our siblings, for our grandparents, aunties and uncles, cousins and extended family. It was a day for everyone to celebrate our marriage, and thus a day for everyone to enjoy. This can be seen as a beautiful thing or a frustrating one. But it is only one day, and some of the things that we were disagreeing on just weren't worth arguing over. Whatever 'sacrifices' this might mean I made, or Luke made, or our parents made, it resulted in a beautiful wedding and a beautiful day for everyone, and more importantly, a beautiful start to our marriage. This is the bigger picture that matters above everything.

Summary of Questions in this Chapter

YOUR STORY BUILDING BLOCK #42: FAMILY INVOLVEMENT

How involved is your family in your wedding?

How do you feel about that level of involvement?

YOUR STORY BUILDING BLOCK #43.A: GUEST LISTS

How will you decide on the size of your guest list?

Who else gets a say in your guest list?

How will you decide whether to invite kids or not?

YOUR STORY BUILDING BLOCK #43.B: GUEST LISTS

What issues are you concerned about that may come up for you in regards to your guest list?

Which way do you think might be the best way to respond?

How comfortable would you be dealing with confrontation about your guest list?

How would you like to be treated if roles were reversed?

What would your [mother/father/other parental figure/role model] advise you to do?

How important is this confronting family member to you?

What are the impacts going to be on the relationship with this person post-wedding?

What if it is a child who admires you who is the one upset that they weren't invited to your wedding—how would you approach a child?

YOUR STORY BUILDING BLOCK #44: EX-PARTNERS AT YOUR WEDDING

How will you approach any exes in your guest list?

What do you feel comfortable with?

How will parents/partners react to this decision?

What extra measures do you feel are necessary to take to keep family peace but ensure comfort at your wedding?

YOUR STORY BUILDING BLOCK #45.A: SEATING PLAN AND ENVIRONMENT CONSIDERATIONS

What might you need to consider for your seating plan that is unique to your wedding?

What factors are important for you?

How do you want to arrange your guests?

What environmental considerations do you need to consider for your wedding venue?

What additional wedding items do you need to organise for these environmental considerations?

YOUR STORY BUILDING BLOCK #45.B: SEATING PLAN AND ENVIRONMENT CONSIDERATIONS

How do you want to work out the seating arrangement?

What method works best for you?

Who else do you need to speak to when creating your seating plan?

YOUR STORY BUILDING BLOCK #46: WHO WILL BE GIVING YOUR WEDDING SPEECHES

Who will be giving speeches at your wedding?

What considerations need to be made in regards to your wedding speech line-up?

What order would you like the speech-givers to give their speeches?

YOUR STORY BUILDING BLOCK #47: WEDDING SPEECH ETIQUETTE

What kind of guidelines might you wish to give to your speech-givers?

Which wedding speeches have you heard and loved in the past?

Which wedding speeches have you heard in the past that you did not like?

How can you approach your speech-givers if you are concerned about their speeches?

If you are majorly concerned, who could you trust to listen to the speeches and ensure they're appropriate, without having to listen to them yourself?

YOUR STORY BUILDING BLOCK #48: MONETARY GIFTS

What is the current state of your household set up, for you and your partner?

How do you feel about asking your guests for monetary gifts?

How big of an issue is this for your circumstances?

Who do you know who will get offended by being asked to give money?

How much does this person's opinion affect you?

Who is immediately involved in this decision (your partner, maybe parents, etc.)?

How do they feel about this?

Which way do you wish to ultimately go?

YOUR STORY BUILDING BLOCK #49: BRIDAL PARTY POLITICS

How well does your bridal party know each other?

How well does your bridal party work together?

Who are you most concerned about?

What can you do to improve your feelings about the bridal party?

How do you feel about getting involved in bridal party tasks in order for things to run smoothly?

How will your relationships be affected post-wedding?

YOUR STORY BUILDING BLOCK #50: GUESTS AND GENERAL FAMILY POLITICS

How much consideration do you wish to give to your guests?

How important is it to you that your guests enjoy your wedding?

Where will be the limit to the extent of consideration you give to your guests?

What are your reasons for insisting on [this argument]?

What are your families' reasons for insisting on [this argument]?

How can you decide what will be worth insisting on, and what will not be?

What are the benefits/consequences of your decision post-wedding?

How will this impact your family relationships?

Further Reading on Family Politics

- ***How to Deal with Difficult People* by Gill Hasson**
A repeat mention, because I really recommend this book. It holds a handful of strategies you can adopt that will help in sticky family political situations.

- ***Confidence* by Tomas Chamorro-Premuzic, PhD**
Despite the title, this book covers a range of topics related to confidence, including relations with other people. Short chapters on narcissism, focusing on others instead of the self, and interpersonal relations show that actually, focusing on others will lead to more success.

Traditions and Generation Gaps

If you're experiencing family politics throughout your wedding planning journey, you might find that a lot of it has come down to differing opinions on traditions. This may be partly due to a generation gap, but nonetheless they'll probably be there. Why they exist isn't something I'm going to look into in too much depth. But from my experience, this was such a prominent area of disagreement, that I warranted it a whole chapter on its own. Traditions and Generation Gaps.

Is there anything we go through in our lives more filled with traditions than a wedding?

Traditions, by definition, are the passing on of customs or beliefs within a group. In this context, the group is your family. Traditions can be family-, cultural- or religion-based. Even if in your everyday life you don't regularly practice the religion you might have been brought up in, or even if you push against your cultural background, you probably will follow some of your family's cultural and religious traditions in your wedding. Why is this so? It might be because a wedding is seen as a formal function, and that calls for such traditional formalities. I don't know the answer to this, and I'm not going to explore this any further here. But it seems to stand for most weddings, that a wedding is the one event in your life that people are most likely to follow traditions.

The thing with traditions is that they stem from times gone before us. As a result, they tend to be outdated and, like many things in the past, they are usually from a time when women weren't given full autonomy. This means that, as a bride in today's day and age, you might not necessarily agree with some of the traditions your family wants you to participate in for your wedding. But because of the fact that they are so strongly embedded in your family history, they can potentially be really hard to fight against. This brings in the generational side of traditions, because when it comes to fighting a tradition, it usually translates into fighting with the generations before you: your parents or your grandparents. It is natural to have differing opinions on traditions compared to the older generations in your family, because you were brought up in different times and tend to see things in a different light. Younger generations are, almost by definition, more current, and thus tend to have more progressive thoughts on traditions that might never have even occurred to previous generations in your family. Even if you are trying to enlighten your family members on new ways to interpret a tradition, they still might find it hard to accept because they have believed in said tradition for such a long time.

It is really hard to undo someone else's belief in a tradition, because it is a BELIEF. Beliefs are not based on hard-facts; they are just something we believe in. It is never something where you can prove who is right and who is wrong. The reasons behind a belief can be discussed, and new and different ways of interpreting a tradition might be understood, but that does not necessarily mean you change what you believe in. For example, imagine believing in a tradition, for decades of your life, for grandparents sometimes up to 80 years' worth of believing, to only have someone much younger than you just come in and tell you no, they don't believe in that tradition for a particular reason.

I think we can all accept that this could be a hard thing to agree with and undo. So, managing different beliefs in traditions for a family event such as a wedding is always going to be a tricky task.

When it comes to traditions, some people are happy just accepting things for what they are, and not questioning why it stands in the first place. Traditions form our status quo, and when anyone tries to shake the status quo, they are also trying to shake our belief system, and that can be unnerving. Only someone who WANTS to change their OWN belief, can work on that and do so. For others, it can be a matter of exposing new understandings to them slowly and consistently, until they warm to a new understanding of a tradition at their own pace, and then they may finally accept it. Still, it's their own decision to accept it. These are people who are open to new information. Other people are stubbornly closed to new information, and until they decide to open up, they will not be willing to budge on a belief. That is their choice.

But, as I have mentioned throughout this book already, you are allowed to agree to disagree. This is a totally reasonable and valid way to move on with an issue. If you have strong characters in your family, this is going to be a tough one. This ties in with your communication skills and your family politics, so all these chapters are related.

As always, before we start, brain dump below any traditions you will be following for your wedding. Include all of them; the ones you're happy to follow, and those you aren't so happy to follow. Include your reasoning behind each one. Also jot down any family clashes you are concerned about when it comes to traditions, and anything else related to generational gaps or traditions that you feel like unloading onto the page before reading this chapter.

Your Story Brain Dump Space

My Story

When it comes to traditions, I question A LOT. I just want to understand why we do certain things, and come to a better-informed decision as to whether I agree with the tradition or not. A wedding was no exception, so when it came to my own, I looked into a lot of the history into the traditions we uphold for weddings, especially when they relate to gender roles and especially when they made me feel uncomfortable. This may also be the case for you, so rest assured—you're not alone in your thoughts.

Engagement and Wedding Rings

Let's start with the proposal. Traditionally, in heterosexual engagements, the male partner proposes to the female with an engagement ring, and it is all, "let's see the ring!" for a while. I have already mentioned in the Mental Health chapter how this can be slightly unfair on the female, as they aren't as mentally prepared for the upcoming marriage as the male is due to the 'surprise'. But it's also unfair on the male. He proposes, she gets an engagement ring to wear proudly and mark herself as engaged, but what does he get? Nothing.

I was not happy with this, so I decided that Luke gets an engagement gift too. I bought him a Tag Heuer watch, something special that he could wear on our wedding day. It was not the equivalent to an engagement ring, i.e., a ring he has to wear all the time, but it was something to mark him as a fiancé, and he happily states it was an engagement gift to everyone who compliments it. Whenever he explains what it was for, more often than not the women think it is a great idea and the men

turn to their partners and say something like, "See? That's fair!".
This little stance against tradition can't really be fought by anyone
in your family, as it doesn't really impact anyone or anything else;
if that's what you want to do then that's fine. Some couples get
engagement rings for both partners too. But maybe you don't
even want an engagement ring; your wedding bands are enough.
You might have avoided the proposal and just mutually decided
to become engaged, in a thought-out decision-making process
about your future together. The tradition where the man typically
does the proposing in a heterosexual relationship is still going
strong, but is slowly being shaken up, and we're hearing more
and more of stories of non-proposals where the couple just
decides to become engaged. Sometimes the female has done the
proposing in a heterosexual relationship. This one still might
generate some judgement, since, as with any change to the status
quo, there might initially be some disapproval and resistance.
Still, getting engaged is such an intimate moment between 2
people, so this tradition is usually unaffected by judgement and
is totally up to you.

If you are reading this book, you are probably already
engaged and beyond this point, so I won't be giving any more
attention to the proposal, but I thought I'd share the above
regardless. For same-sex relationships, this tradition doesn't
apply, so they get to choose how they wish to proceed when
becoming engaged (more on same-sex couples later).

YOUR STORY BUILDING BLOCK #51: EQUAL ENGAGEMENT GIFTS
What do you think about both partners in the relationship getting an engagement ring/gift?
What does your partner think?
What have you chosen to do?

Back to rings though: another point on the engagement ring is WHO picks the design. This is totally up to you. Again, you might be beyond this point, but you also might not be; not all proposals involve a ring. Some people propose with another piece of jewellery first (or something else), and allow their surprised partner to design their ring themselves at a later date.

I had always told Luke that I wanted him to choose the ring. I knew if I had to choose it, it would've been an absolute headache. I really didn't know where to start. And knowing myself, I would have overthought everything, second-guessed certain details, etc. So, I told Luke I want him to choose it. I gave him no direction other than I would like detail in the ring. Luke has always had good taste when it comes to choosing gifts and jewellery for me, so I trusted he would do a good job. He actually ended up designing it himself, and I absolutely love the ring. It means more to me knowing that he designed it and put thought into it for me. This is the traditional route, the man choosing the ring, but my choice to let Luke choose has got nothing to do with that. If I had wanted a say in the design, I would've been granted this. Not everyone agrees with my reason though; I've met women who want a say in the design of the ring, because it is a ring that they are going to wear for the rest of their lives, so why can't they have a say in the design?! Another reason might be that you don't trust your partner's taste in jewellery, or they have a different taste to yours. Whatever the reason, they are all completely valid and you can absolutely choose whatever you wish—but you will need to communicate your wishes with your partner, to ensure that the two of you are on the same page and one of you doesn't go ahead on one particular route.

Whichever way you choose, one thing you can do with your partner is play games in jewellery shop windows. It's quite fun to do to see what your partner thinks you'd like. Stand with your partner in front of a jewellery shop window—you don't have to go in—and each of you picks what ring you, the reader, would like. Pick the ring in your head and don't say it out loud. Once you've picked, then let your partner reveal what they picked for you. You can then reveal your pick, and see if they match, discuss your choices and have a giggle. You can then swap and let your partner have a turn. You can even do this with other pieces of jewellery, or other items altogether. It's one of those 'let's see how our tastes match!' games you can do with your partner.

YOUR STORY BUILDING BLOCK #52: WHO IS PICKING THE RING DESIGN

Who is picking your engagement and wedding ring design?
What have you discussed with your partner?
If you're opting for your partner to choose the design, what specific requirements or guidelines do you wish to give your partner?
How do you and your partner feel about your final decision?

There are also traditions for the actual DESIGN of an engagement ring. The ring has been the choice symbol of marriage for centuries for its circular nature, a long-time symbol of eternity. The indestructible nature of the diamond renders the gemstone symbolic of the indestructible nature of the marriage[3], and thus we have the stereotypical and traditional diamond engagement ring. While the ring is still the most recognisable symbol of marriage, more and more people are exploring

---

[3] Church, R. 2017. *Rings.* Victoria and Albert Museum, UK.

different styles and designs for the ring, to make them individual to the wearer. All cuts and shapes, all different types and colours of gemstones, are being explored with. For example, the design of Luke's wedding ring was inspired by the wavy patterns you see scraped into gelati at gelati shops. I love this fact, and so do others. We also have a relative who has an engagement ring that has a black onyx stone instead of a diamond. I've generally found people are quite open to these new ways of interpreting the design of a wedding ring or an engagement ring, so this is a refreshing and positive way that traditions can evolve and stay current. It is also common to buy ring sets, where the engagement ring and the wedding ring fit together and sit on your finger, matching up and going together nicely. You can get some sets where there is also a matching partner's ring. And honestly, while the ring is the most common symbol of marriage, who said it had to be a ring in the first place? There are literally so many choices, so get creative and make it yours.

YOUR STORY BUILDING BLOCK #53: THE RING DESIGN ITSELF

> *If you haven't organised your engagement ring yet, what do you want for your engagement ring?*
> *What do you want for your wedding ring?*
> *What do you NOT want for your wedding ring? What design features don't you like?*
> *Where can you look for inspiration?*
> *How can you narrow your options down?*
> *How do you want your ring and your partner's ring to match, if at all?*

The next thing that comes into the rings, is the hand you wear them on. Traditionally, in most of the Western world, the ring is worn on the 4th finger of the left-hand, because it is believed there is a vein that runs from this finger directly to the heart, another symbolic gesture to the love in your marriage. In some countries though, people wear the wedding bands on the right-hand, as religiously or culturally the left-hand is seen as unclean and untrustworthy. As a left-hander myself, I know this first-hand. When I was starting to pick up pencils and draw as a toddler, I recall my grandparents trying to change the hand I was using, putting the pencil into my right-hand, to no avail (eventually they gave up). Many religions and cultures have a superstition about the left-side, and as part of this belief wear wedding rings on the right-hand. There are other reasons for right-hand ring wearing as well; some left-handers wear their ring on the right hand so that they don't damage it through extra wear, while some wear their rings on the right-hand when their partner has passed away. Some people don't even wear their rings on their finger; they wear them on chains around their neck, or, if you are like my father, their profession would damage the ring, so they don't wear their ring at all.

YOUR STORY BUILDING BLOCK #54: THE HAND YOU'LL BE WEARING YOUR RINGS ON

> *What hand will you wear your wedding ring on, if at all?*
> *What hand will your partner be wearing their wedding ring on, if at all?*
> *How do you feel about these decisions?*

Now, if your family has a ring that is passed down through generations, but you don't like the ring, this is where you might have your first generational clash. You might need to bring this topic into any marriage conversations you have with your partner early on so that you can minimise any disappointments. It depends on how receptive and flexible your families, *and* your partner, are. That ring might come with a lot of baggage; there is sentiment involved, a strong tradition, and personal tastes that can be offended. Maybe a grandparent was gifting it to you in person, and you also have their feelings that might be hurt if you don't accept it. Maybe the person who was the original owner of the ring has now deceased, and the ring is even more sentimental as it symbolises them. This is all usually just for one side of the family by the way. For example, say Luke was proposing to me with a ring passed down through his side of the family. I would feel a lot of pressure, and yet the ring wouldn't necessarily mean the same to me as it did to Luke, because I didn't necessarily know the person, and I am not as attached to the family sentiment. This kind of consideration needs to go into a ring that is passed down through a family. It can be a really beautiful and romantic gesture, but it can also be an extremely loaded one. I have been gifted a ring that belonged to Luke's late grandmother, and I have also been gifted a ring by my own Nonna. Neither of the rings were related to our marriage, but the passing down tradition was still kept, and I continue to wear them on occasion. This could potentially be an alternative for you to suggest to your partner and family if this is a concern for you. There are many other solutions as well, such as having a ring re-made.

YOUR STORY BUILDING BLOCK #55: PASSING DOWN OF FAMILY RINGS

> *How do you feel about rings that are passed down in your family?*
>
> *How open are your families in discussing this topic?*
>
> *What other ways could you suggest to make the*

families happy but still end up with a ring that you are happy with?

Where does your partner sit on the issue?

When can you talk about this with your partner?

Ultimately, the engagement ring, and the wedding rings to follow, come down to what feels right for you and your partner. You may choose to have engagement rings for both you and your partner; you may choose to go traditional or create your own style; and you can choose which finger you wear your ring on, or how you wear it if at all, depending on your everyday lifestyle. The ring has little impact on others outside of the couple, so it really is just what feels most comfortable for you two. You are the ones who will hopefully have them for the rest of your lives, so you need to be happy with it! But as important as the ring is, remember the bigger picture: it doesn't matter what your ring is, it is what it represents—the marriage—that is most important.

Traditional Stereotypes

Traditional stereotypes can be a subtle one, because unless you're consciously aware of them, they can slide under the radar as 'normal'. As you have been made aware, I was the call centre for the entire operation that was our wedding. This was, as you now know, mostly due to the fact that Luke was living in New Zealand and literally couldn't take part in the same way I was. But despite this extra layer, I did find, that as the bride-to-be in a heterosexual marriage, the majority of the pressure for the wedding was on me, even if Luke had been more present. In the UK, this is also true; in 98% of weddings the bride is the most heavily involved in the wedding, with the groom falling second at 81%[4]. The bride is almost 20% more involved than the groom. According to the same report, the second most involved in the wedding are the women of the wedding: mothers of the couple and the bridesmaids. This trend feeds the expectation that the women do more, care more and are more responsible for wedding stuff, and this in-turn feeds the trend. It's a feedback loop, a catch-22. As a result, there's a lot more pressure on the ladies when planning a wedding. There are also a lot of traditional stereotypes about weddings that still fall on the bride. In conversations throughout the year leading up to our wedding, people kept referring to our wedding day as '*my* day', and I would always correct them, saying, 'No, it's actually *our* day'. There was also this assumption that I was ruling the planning because I was the bride, not because I was in the correct country, and that Luke was second to me. That is so not true: Luke had a lot of input and sway in the decision-making, and if it weren't for the separate countries, he would've been even more involved. But how many mainstream wedding movies have you seen that revolve around the groom as the main person for his wedding? I can't think of any. All I can think of are the likes of *Bride Wars*, *Bridesmaids* and *27 Dresses*. Movies like these show the ridiculous demands brides supposedly place on people because 'it's *my* wedding!'. *Bride Wars* and *Bridesmaids* also show the supposedly competitive nature that comes out of brides and bridesmaids when it comes to weddings. Sure, these are just movies and are exaggerated to entertain us, but they feed a culture of wedding judgment that we are all part of and guilty of. Judging a bride's dress on what we did and did not like about it, comparing the bridesmaids' dresses, and picking on the

---

[4] 'The UK Wedding Report 2018' by Bridebook.co.uk

engagement ring. I conclude: from personal experience and from mainstream pop culture, there is definitely more pressure on the bride than the groom.

These female bride stereotypes are so mainstream I'm going to class them as a tradition now[5]. I quote Ross from *Friends* season 7, episode 2, to illustrate the traditional attitude about the groom's role in a heterosexual wedding, "All you have to do is show up and say the right name". This is 20 years old now but still, this stereotype is still present for a lot of us and is so not ok. I still speak to women who imply their partner doesn't care about this or that detail of their wedding, simply because he's the male. Between Luke and I, Luke also had dreams about what his wedding would be like, and he also had a strong stance on aspects of the wedding. I would say I let Luke get more of what he wanted for the wedding because it meant more to him, he knew what he wanted more than I did, and his happiness meant more to me than some of the detail on our wedding day. And *because* of the fact he was in New Zealand, I made an extra effort to include him in the wedding preparations; I didn't want him to feel like he was removed from it all and had missed out on such a big milestone in his life. I've spoken to other men who have dreams and ideas for their weddings, and I'm sure there are plenty of other men out there as well. But while people *theoretically* know that technically men are *of course* involved in their wedding, the overlying discussion, jokes and comments all still suggest otherwise. I don't even know if people are even conscious of it, because it is so instilled in our everyday language and society. It's no surprise a stereotyped character like Bridezilla

---

[5] Ingraham, C. 1999, *White Weddings: Romancing Heterosexuality in Popular Culture,* Routledge, NY. The whole book really, but more specifically, p133.

exists. It is supposed to be comical, but it is also insulting. That's another catch-22, because actually it's the jokes and the pressure on the bride that can potentially cause her to crack, which feeds the Bridezilla stereotype and proves it even more so, which allows it to remain part of society and continue to feed back to brides, and around in circles we go.

If you genuinely enjoy the activities and traditions that fill the stereotypical bridal box, then, by all means, ignore this section. Don't feel guilty for enjoying it if you do; just become aware that that is indeed your choice, and that that choice is truly yours. But if you are a modern-day woman, who's interested in gender equality and are soon to be a bride, you may be very aware of these little issues, and they can definitely get to you or make you feel uncomfortable. Being aware of them in advance can help you feel not so blindsided when they come along.

Another traditional and stereotypical wedding event is the Kitchen Tea. Traditionally, this is a females-only event to give the bride gifts to set up her kitchen. Today, it is no longer *her* kitchen. Both you and your partner, whatever your genders, will be using that kitchen. If your intentions in your married life are to be in this role, that you will be the main kitchen user and can't wait until you have your own kitchen, then you might see this as a beautiful tradition, and are looking forward to all the kitchen tea shenanigans and games about to come your way. But regardless of whether you agree with it or not, this tradition is one that stems from the woman-as-housewife days of the past. You may be told, as I was, that you're overreacting and reading into things, but this partly goes back to people not being comfortable with you shaking the status quo. When it comes to your own wedding, you deserve to speak up about anything that makes you feel uncomfortable. For me, it was a simple request to my bridesmaids to plan a 'bridal shower' rather than a 'kitchen tea', which changed the focus just enough to avoid the stereotype. People will not necessarily see things the same way you have, especially if they have happily accepted traditional stereotypes for what they are. For this section, I do want to make the call for more research into weddings, because in an age where almost everything has been researched, it is surprisingly impressive how weddings have escaped being studied thoroughly.

It is up to you on how you wish to approach people who make comments to you and these gender-based, traditional, stereotyped assumptions. It can be as simple as correcting "my day" to "our day", or—gently—questioning the things people say, making them aware of what they've just said in a way that doesn't attack them. Humour might be a good tool to use here. This might depend on how close you are with them, otherwise you might just wish to ignore them. But definitely do not accept being called Bridezilla. You don't deserve that. A bride is allowed to be upset or angry and not immediately be dubbed Bridezilla. Any other year and you'd just be upset. The same needs to go for your wedding planning period.

You might deal with traditional stereotypes differently, and you might experience other traditional stereotypes that I have not mentioned here. Again, you might also just love the traditions and want to lap it all up and enjoy it while it lasts! Traditional stereotypes, if they do pose an issue to you, are definitely tricky to navigate, because usually they're lots of little subtle things as opposed to big obvious ones. It's harder to talk about these smaller things without being told you're overreacting.

YOUR STORY BUILDING BLOCK #56: TRADITIONAL STEREOTYPES

How do you feel about gender-based traditional stereotypes?

271

What traditional stereotypes have you noticed during your wedding planning period?

What traditional stereotypes are you comfortable with?

What traditional stereotypes are you not comfortable with?

How do you want to handle situations when traditional stereotypes you don't agree with are brought up?

What might be some of the consequences of standing up to any traditional stereotypes you experience?

How comfortable are you in going against the grain and potentially standing out?

It's ok to accept a traditional stereotype for your wedding, even if you don't agree with it. This way, you don't have to compromise your beliefs. What traditional stereotypes are you content accepting as part of your wedding, but don't agree with?

The Wedding Dress

I can only speak from my experience of my own Western-style wedding, so this section is particularly related to this culture. But the bare bones of the arguments can still be relatable for your wedding attire, regardless of your family's cultural background.

In Western-style weddings, there is so much hype when it comes to the wedding dress. Everyone knows what a suit looks like, but the wedding dress? It could be anything. It is even more exciting these days because a lot of brides are pushing the boundaries of what a wedding dress can be, so you never know what you are going to see when you rock up as a guest to a wedding.

Traditionally, it is a big white puffy thing. The princess cut I believe it is called. This is a nod to the bride 'feeling like a princess' on her big day, and some brides will have a tiara to go that one step further to mimic this fairy-tale wedding. The wedding dress is typically white to represent the bride's purity (a.k.a. the bride's virginity). Traditionally wedding dresses also haven't been too revealing either, because a bride needs to be 'modest' in her pure state. Symbolism aside, if you like this style of dress, then you won't have any issues. But if you don't like this style, then you may find yourself up against your family.

I was one of those brides. I didn't want the big white wedding dress for a variety of reasons. I went shopping for my wedding dress with my aunty, my mum and Luke's mum. These were the only 3 people who saw my dress; everyone else saw it on the day of the wedding. This is also a little tradition that lots of brides follow; the dress is a surprise. It fuels the wedding dress hype further, but also creates a little fun. I was fine with that part. I tried on about 10 dresses, before I chose one. The dress I chose was quite a bit further from white than I initially set out for; the tag said 'Moscato' colour, like the dessert wine. It was a sort of dusty pink champagne colour; definitely not white. It was also strapless, and came to about mid-way up my back. My mum was initially not too pleased with this; she thought it was a beautiful dress on me, but she had expected I would go for a less revealing dress and one that was not so far from white as I had chosen. We had a tiny disagreement in the shop. My mum had simply arrived to each of the fittings with a certain expectation, and reality was not meeting that expectation, so she was a little thrown. This is completely normal. I had my aunty and my mother-in-law on my side with this dress, which cheekily helped. It took her a few moments to come around, but the more she thought about it, the more she accepted it. The dress was truly beautiful, and because of its unusual shade, it made it even more of a special stand-out. It was not a typical colour for a wedding dress, but it suited me and my skin tone perfectly.

That is one downside to beliefs and expectations; they can discolour your view of what is otherwise a beautiful wedding outfit. Fortunately for me, my mum was open enough and came around very quickly. But we have all watched movies and TV shows like *Say Yes to the Dress*, where mums, dads, grandparents, or even siblings and friends can have really strong and dominating opinions about the dress, and let those get in the way of giving their approval of it. Not that, as brides-to-be, we *need* approval, but when you come out glowing because you love the dress you're in, and your family's reactions are negative, it can kill the vibe for you. It is totally natural to want your immediate loved ones to love your dress as well. When you've found the right dress for you, sounds cheesy but, it will feel right. It's the kind of dress that you come out of the change room smiling and glowing in, and those around you can tell you feel good in it. It's hard to say no to this feeling, but if they do, give your family a little time and they might just come around. This comes back to the Communication chapter and how to approach disagreements; step away from the disagreement and let the dress sit on people's minds for a little bit. Take photos, go home and mull over them. Sometimes your family's critiques of a dress can be legitimate; if you're high on wedding dress shopping and caught up in the excitement of it, you might not see that initially. You might feel they're just being opposed to you for the sake of being opposed. So, time for you to mull over any critiques might be helpful for your decision process too.

Just like the rings earlier, who said your wedding dress needs to be a dress? Who said it needs to be a muted hue of a colour? This would be a big tradition to change, but your wedding day outfit could be a total change up from tradition—bold and colourful dresses, or pant suits and other outfits. Not all cultures have the big white dress either of course. Many already have beautifully coloured outfits, but maybe, if this is your culture, actually you do want the muted tones instead and are struggling with the reverse? You may shock a few guests, particularly if you aren't telling people what you're choosing to do, but that could be part of the fun! Don't expect everyone to be ready to accept this, but ultimately, your wedding day outfit needs to feel right for you. You need to feel great in it, regardless of what others think.

YOUR STORY BUILDING BLOCK #57: WEDDING DAY OUTFIT CHOICE

What will you be wearing for your wedding day?

How many outfits will you be wanting/needing for your wedding day?

Who will you be taking with you to shop for your wedding day outfit, if anyone?

Who else gets a say in your wedding day outfit?

How open are they to different wedding day outfit styles?

How revealing is too revealing for you?

How revealing is too revealing for your parents/partner/grandparents?

What will happen if you and the people you are shopping with disagree on an outfit?

How will you resolve any disapprovals on your chosen wedding day outfit?

The other traditional bit about the wedding dress get-up is the veil. Of all the reasons I could find for why we have veils in weddings, not one of them is relevant to the 21st Century. I couldn't find any credible sources for these reasons since, as I've already mentioned, there is not a lot of research out there. The veil seems to mean different things to different cultures at different times in human history. Reasons why range from, again, representing the bride's modesty and purity, to keeping the groom or bride from running away at the sight of their partner in arranged marriages. Truly romantic stuff.

YOUR STORY BUILDING BLOCK #58: THE VEIL

What decision have you made with regards to a veil?
How do you feel about the veil?
How much say do you have in choosing this part of your wedding outfit?
Who else is this truly impacting?

The last part of the wedding dress ensemble I will mention here is the garter. The garter is a stretchy bit of lacey lingerie originally meant to hold up stockings. At the wedding reception, it can be tradition for the groom to go under the bride's dress, slide the garter off the bride's leg, and blindly throw it into a crowd of all the single men in attendance. The garter is supposedly symbolic of 2 things. The first is it's a sign of the consummation of the marriage, and the second is it's meant to bring good luck to whoever catches it. In the distant past, guests used to try and tear off a piece of the wedding dress after the marriage ceremony to bring them good luck[6]. The garter throw is a less violent derivative of this. The female version of receiving good luck is the throwing of the bouquet. From my experience, no one is

---

[6] Bridebox Wedding Albums (2015) "Everything You Need to Know about the Wedding Garter". [http://www.bridebox.com/blog/everything-need-know-wedding-garter/]

likely to object to your decision to have or not have these traditional activities at your wedding; it usually means there's more time for dancing instead.

YOUR STORY BUILDING BLOCK #59: THE GARTER AND BOUQUET THROW

How do you feel about the garter?

What decision have you made with regards to a garter?

What decision have you made with regards to the throwing of the bouquet?

What other games/activities would you like to have at your wedding instead, if any?

So far these have been Western-style wedding traditions, and are the only ones I'm truly familiar with. There are of course others out there; you may already be thinking of some that are related to your own culture. Instead of simply taking them in your stride, be curious and see where they stem from. A deeper understanding of why something is the way it is will help you consciously choose and form your own wedding story.

Cultures and Religious Traditions

Weddings within the same families *tend* to be somewhat similar. This is the case for weddings in my family, and when you have weddings as frequently as we have, you start to expect a certain standard of wedding when you attend them. Fortunately, Luke's family is quite similar to ours, so expectations were all on the same page, and the majority of our guests were pretty familiar with how a Dujmovic or Morelli wedding would go. This in a way was a blessing in disguise, because I know of plenty of families who, let's say, do not mesh as well with each other. This *tends* to happen when families come from different cultural backgrounds. The more different the cultures, the greater the differences in wedding expectations. One side are used to weddings of a certain kind, while the other side are used to weddings of another kind. This just is what it is. Furthermore, particularly with older family members who have more established beliefs, the kind of weddings they are used to may align with their personal preference now; they may not be interested in experiencing other kinds of weddings. They might like things just as they are. All they want to do is attend a wedding where they are familiar with the proceedings and know what to expect. Anything different and they won't be pleased with the uncertainty. In this situation, while you aren't going to be able to please everyone, you can't blame anyone either. Extend understanding towards their experience in these instances.

Some families openly embrace new experiences, and a culturally mixed wedding is an opportunity to do so. But I have been to weddings where, for example, one side of the family were not familiar with allocated seating, and just tried to sit anywhere, causing some chaos. I have been to weddings where it was VERY clear that the bride's family were not fans of the groom's family, and I have been to weddings where one or both sides of the family bring in cultural entertainment of one form or another, and everyone completely embraces everyone, dances and celebrates together.

You can't control how people are going to react; this you will have to accept. It will be beyond your control. When it comes to cultures, I have found that when I have been open and interested in the other culture, when I have made the effort to get to know new family members and embraced the cultural difference, that is when all has gone smoothly. When things don't go smoothly, instead of having an awkward moment, the best way to respond is with a smile and a laugh. Going back to *My Big Fat Greek Wedding*, cultural bumps can make for funny moments, and this movie shows how you can do that. On the wedding day, if something does not go according to plan due to cultural misunderstandings, be understanding and see the lighter side. Whoever misunderstood may feel silly or embarrassed as well, so lightening the mood and showing understanding will help everyone feel more at home with what is otherwise a new experience for everyone.

YOUR STORY BUILDING BLOCK #60: CULTURAL DIFFERENCES

What family clashes are you concerned about at your wedding?

What is in your control when it comes to these family clashes?

What is NOT in your control?

How similar are you and your partner's families?

How do they get along?

How can you change your perception on family culture clashes to make it more enjoyable for you on your wedding day?

If the couple getting married are from 2 different religions, then this may also include some religious differences. Many weddings exist where 2 marriage ceremonies are required, so that the newlywed couple is recognised as married in both of their respective religions. There is more paperwork involved, and if you are happy to oblige this extra step, then you'll have no problems. But even if you are not, this might be a hard one to fight against if your family insists. What are you going to do? You might just oblige to make your family happy, because maybe you feel the alternative is not worth your energy.

The reverse might also be true: maybe you want to get married and recognised in your particular religion, but your family or religious house won't allow it. Even within my own religion, Roman Catholic, different churches seem to have different rules as to who they allow to marry within a particular church. It depends on the discretion of the priest at that church. Unless you want to go up against your religious house, there might not be anything you can do right now (you never know how the future will change though; you could be part of that process too, who knows!). This also depends on how religious you and your families are, and how strong they practice their religion, if at all.

YOUR STORY BUILDING BLOCK #61: RELIGIONS
What is yours and your partner's religious situation?
How do you feel about your religious situation?
What extra religious factors do you need to consider?
What could you do to please your family and still be happy (i.e. a win-win scenario)?

Walking Down the Aisle

This tradition stems from times gone by when women were not autonomous figures. A father walking his daughter down the aisle and handing her over to her soon-to-be husband, symbolises the daughter as the property of her father, and, once married, transferring to the property of her husband. After all, it's called 'giving away' for a reason.

Women have a long and hard history of fighting to become autonomous, but we have come a long way. In most Western countries it is no longer the case that women are 'given away' as property from their fathers to their soon-to-be husbands. So why do we still engage in a tradition that represents that?

People have been doing this tradition in their families for years and have just accepted it for *what* it is, and not *why* it is. My family does not think I am the property of my father, or my husband. Your family probably knows that too. They know that we aren't anyone's property. They just think that walking down the aisle is a beautiful father-daughter dream. You might even think that too. Don't feel bad about this if you do like this tradition. But there is a general lack of understanding in why we have all the traditions that we have in a wedding, so it's good to know why something is the way it is. Increase your awareness of what you're doing.

If you want to change up this tradition, there's a few ways you can do so:

1. You could have both of your parents walk you down the aisle; this takes away from the male ownership aspect. This also gives your mum a role in the wedding (something that is otherwise generally formally non-existent).

2. You could walk down the aisle by yourself; you and your partner are both consenting adults in your marriage, no one needs to be 'given away'.

3. Both your parents and your partner's parents could do some sort of giving away manoeuvre, seeing this as a beautiful parent-child tradition rather than a gender-based one.

4. Both you and your partner walk down the aisle, either separately or together.

5. Have no aisle at all!

Before you make a decision, there is someone else who needs to be considered here: your dad or other father-figure who'd be walking you down the aisle. The walking your daughter down the aisle dream is a dream of a lot of fathers, whether they voice these dreams or not. My dad would've dreamed about this moment since the day I was born. How could I say my dreams were more important than my dad's 20+ year old dream? How could I deny my dad his dream just to make my own come true? I know my dad doesn't think I am his property. I am also his only daughter, so he would only get the chance for his dream to come true with me. What needs to be achieved here is a compromise. My dad needed to be a part of this tradition, but I wanted the male ownership aspect removed. I chose to go with Option Number 1. At the end of the day, both my parents have raised me, so both my parents can walk me down the aisle. Otherwise, my mum doesn't really get any role in the wedding, and that didn't really sit well with me either. My mum has done absolutely everything she possibly could for me, and she deserves to be a part of the wedding just as much as my dad. This tradition made my dad's dream come true, but ended up being made even more special by sharing it with my mum. This is obviously based on my circumstances. You will need to consider yours, and have a conversation with your father-figure if he is present and expecting to be participating in this tradition.

YOUR STORY BUILDING BLOCK #62: WALKING DOWN THE AISLE

What are you choosing to do in regards to walking down the aisle?
Who is walking you down the aisle in your wedding?
How do you feel about this?

What options are available to you?
Who else do you need to consider in this decision?
How might they feel about this decision?
What can you do to come to a decision that all those involved agree on?

Bridal Party

There are other people walking down the aisle at the wedding which can cause a bit of drama on the traditional front, and they are the bridal party. This is not one you would immediately pick, and one that unexpectedly came up for us, so chances are it could for you too.

Normally in a bridal party, you have several bridesmaids to support the bride, and several groomsmen to support the groom. One of the bridesmaids is considered a Maid of Honour, and similarly in amongst the groomsmen a Best Man, with each bridesmaid paired with a groomsman.

In our wedding, we had 4 bridesmaids and 4 groomsmen to begin with. I decided to have 2 Maids of Honour, which shook traditions up a little bit but was accepted across the board. But as mentioned earlier, one of our groomsmen pulled out. This meant that we were left with 4 bridesmaids and 3 groomsmen. Luke and I were cool with this; the Best Man will escort the 2 Maids of Honour, and the remaining will pair up just fine.

Our parents had a field day. They could not understand how this was going to work. How unsymmetrical the bridal party will look! And on and on they went. This went on all year. It was driving us nuts. This was the touchiest topic for our family for a LONG TIME. It seemed such a little detail to Luke and me, and yet, of all the issues throughout our wedding, this was the one that got dragged out the most. In the end, in the last month before the wedding, Luke surprisingly flipped and decided on asking someone else. As far as I'm aware—and I sure did double check—he was not pressured by the parents into asking. I knew he had had a few friends that he had been trying to decide between for a while at the beginning of the year. So, when he came to me and said he had decided to ask a fourth groomsmen, I was cool with it. And FINALLY, the parents got off our backs about it.

Before that experience it didn't even occur to me that an even bridal party could be a tradition. But now that I think about it, I don't think I have ever attended a wedding where there *hasn't* been a matching number of bridesmaids and groomsmen. But other than symmetry, there really isn't any reason why you can't!

There are other standards for the bridal party that seem to go unsaid. That is, until you start to stray from them. For example, some couples mix the genders of bridesmaids and groomsmen—who said only females can be bridesmaids and males the groomsmen? Traditionally, the bridal party are of similar age or generation to the marrying couple, but who said you couldn't have parents or older friends and role model figures in your life in your bridal party, or children? For couples who already have children, they are often included in the bridal party as well. Traditionally, the bridesmaids all wear the same style and colour dress, and the groomsmen all the same suit. Who said this still needs to stand? Who says there's a set number of people in your bridal party? Who says the bridal party needs to go in a particular order? Shake these traditions up! Your creativity with the bridal party is as broad as your imagination, or alternatively, you might like to just stick to the classic traditions and not over-think it.

If you do decide to shake things up, prepare for any

potential turmoil from your family (or even friends). They may be super supportive or passive, and not mind at all about your ideas. They may even embrace them. Or they could be like our parents and bug you. Such a simple detail to us—having an uneven bridal party—seemed so minute, and yet our family couldn't drop it. Even if they didn't enforce it upon us, they let their opinions be known and gave Luke and me this constant nagging pressure. Fortunately, it never got ugly, and was kept light-hearted or disguised as a joke. But it can still be frustrating to work with. This is where you can share some of the points in this book and let your parents, or anyone else who is trying to influence your decision know, that by accepting your decision doesn't mean they agree with it. If it has no majorly detrimental or unsafe impacts on anyone else, then this might be enough to show them how you can both deal with the disagreement with maturity.

YOUR STORY BUILDING BLOCK #63: BRIDAL PARTY TRADITIONS

How many people make up your bridal party?

How do you feel about the group line-up?

What issues are you facing with your bridal party line-up?

What other bridal party ideas do you wish to do with your bridal party?

How are those closest to you accepting this?

What makes these decisions worth it?

How does your partner/parents/bridal party feel?

How best can you approach those who aren't accepting your bridal party decisions?

Surname Change

I have already discussed the anxiety a surname change can cause in <u>Mental Health</u>, but here I am going to talk about the tradition.

Heterosexual marriages have such ingrained social norms and traditions when it comes to a surname change. Same-sex marriages are relatively new in human history, and when you are treading a new path, you also get to create new rules. Where same-sex marriages are legal, the new rule is, they can do what they want, without the same scrutiny as a heterosexual couple surname-change. Think about it. If 2 people of the same sex get married, which one is the one who changes their surname? It doesn't matter as much who it is, because either of them can change their name. Both get the freedom *FROM* choice and both get the freedom *OF* choice. There is no real social norm to follow yet. But if you think about a heterosexual couple, you automatically assume it is the female who either will or will not change their surname. The male does not need to face the issue at all. The fact that the female *has* to choose in the first place is, to me, the issue. The females only get the freedom *OF* choice, and not the freedom *FROM* choice. I was surprisingly constantly asked, "What's your new surname going to be?". Um, excuse me, this was 2017. Why are you still assuming I am taking my husband's surname? I thought the more appropriate question would be, "ARE you changing your surname?", and, if yes, then, "What's it going to be?". Truth was I had not fully decided yet at that point; I was still trying to work it out.

When the time comes to deal with the changing of a surname, there are several routes you can choose from:
- You could take the traditional route and take your husband's surname
- Your husband could take your surname

- You could both hyphenate your surnames
- Your future children's surnames (if you intend on having children) could be hyphenated, but your partner's and yours could remain the same
- You could merge your partner's surname and your surname together to create a new surname, that you, your partner and any potential children will adopt, or just the children

What other options can you think of?

These were the options I considered myself. It took me a year and a half to work out how I felt about this and to finally decide on what to do. Even though I 'chose' this, I don't really *feel* like I had much of a choice. There was a clear favourite amongst those around me. It was really important to me to keep Morelli, because it was MY NAME dammit. I am still part of my Morelli family and I didn't want to lose this. I chose the best option available to me, and that was to keep my 'Morelli' surname as my middle name.

The surname decision you choose is up to you, but if you're in the 'against', it can be a hard one, especially if you're not in agreement with your partner. That can hurt both of you. If you have no dramas with the traditional option—taking your husband's name—then you probably won't have a problem, it will just be a matter of getting used to it. If you and your partner agree on a choice, again, then you probably won't have a problem. Any doubts or panic moments that pop up will be a lot easier to deal with because you'll be able to support each other through them if you're in the decision together. But if you and your partner have different ideas on this, that is where things might get sticky. Luke and I had many discussions, doubts, and me a few tears stressing about this decision. Luke completely understood where I was coming from, and the more time passes the more he understands the issue too. The more women who speak up about this, the more men will hear it, and it will become more understanding all round. More progressive decisions will start to be made, as they already have been. I've spoken to couples who have chosen all of the abovementioned options. Depending on how you look at the surname change, you might see it as a solely personal decision just to be made by you, or one that is jointly made with your partner. At the end of the day, the decision, however you choose to decide, will impact both you and your partner. If anyone around chooses to share their judgement or disapproval to you on a progressive decision, chances are they'll do so to your partner as well. Your partner will be the sole person who you'll want on board with the final decision, so talk to them and discuss the options that are available to you. You and your partner are going to be together in a marriage, and it's important that you gain each other's support on matters that are important to either of you.

YOUR STORY BUILDING BLOCK #64: CHANGING UP THE SURNAME CHANGE

How open is your partner to discussing the surname change?

How progressive are you and your partner?

How supportive is your partner on your decision in regards to your surname?

How comfortable are you dealing with the thoughts of others on the matter?

Accepted Traditions

I've so far mentioned some of the traditions that you might struggle with—and I stress *might*—but there are some really beautiful traditions out there too. There will be some that you want to fully embrace, or even start yourself. It is, after all, a wedding, and in general, a rather formal event in your life. It's almost a definite that there will be traditions going on. For example, in our family, it is incredibly likely that at any given wedding there will be traditions about food. For our guests, we had canapes with pre-dinner drinks, then a 4-course sit-down meal, dessert being served with coffee and platters of wedding cake. Open bar all night. See, in our family, we would rather our guests roll out, instead of going to the McDonald's drive-thru on the way home because they left our wedding hungry. Not feeding the guests well is probably the biggest insult you could give in our family. Luke and I barely had a choice here, but we love our food, so this tradition wasn't a problem for us.

YOUR STORY BUILDING BLOCK #65: ACCEPTED TRADITIONS

> *What traditions are unique to your family?*
> *Which traditions are you happy following?*
> *What traditions are you proud of?*
> *What new family traditions do you wish to start?*
> *What will you need to organise to start this tradition?*

Traditions are tricky, especially if you try to fight some of the ones from within your family. It is all well and good to just say, "Do what you want!", "It's your wedding!", or "It doesn't matter what they think!". Family is more complicated than that, and these sayings are easier said than done sometimes. It's not possible to just do what you want for your wedding and not be impacted by what your family thinks, especially if you are close. Some traditions you can choose to be passive about, because the alternative—fighting against—would be draining and not worth your energy, nor worth the hurt it would cause your family relationships. I have said it before, and I will say it again: **it may be yours and your partner's wedding day, but it is not a day just for you two**. And this is where the balance between letting the day be enjoyable for others as well as for you comes in.

Weddings, from my experience, are changing. Slowly, but surely. More and more they are becoming 'modernised'. We tried to do that as much as we could within our wedding, without going so far as making all the wedding formalities unrecognisable and unfamiliar to the rest of the family. The thing with traditions is that, they will take time to evolve. So, every little action you can take to help that process counts, even if it is tiny. That little action you took will make it easier for the next couple getting married in your family to take another little progressive step, and slowly over the years, your family's weddings will evolve to more updated traditions, ones that are unrecognisable from the current ones. Changing traditions requires a transition period, so that you don't shock the system of all the little worlds all your guests live in. We can communicate and educate, but any change will always take time.

The important thing to remember is to not attack others' choices. If a place of understanding can't be reached, then all you can do is respect people's right to their own opinion. So, if you are discussing these kinds of topics with others, keep the discussion open, be aware of your body language and tone of voice, and enjoy a mature examination of the tradition from all sides.

Suggestion Box

1. COMMUNICATE.

It has been the key to everything so far hasn't it? Good communication leads to understanding, and understanding leads to new perspectives and changes in beliefs. When you clash with different generations in your family, or disagree with some of the traditions, a cool, well-formed argument will be one that has been explained clearly. This means explaining your reasons plus how you feel about them. If you are given the opportunity to do this, then return the favour and listen to the other person's side too. Being open and listening are key here.

2. BE GENTLE AND BE PATIENT.

The key players in your life may all have different belief systems to you, and it is even more likely to be different between those who are of different generations to you. Beliefs are hard to change in someone else. There are 2 steps to changing one of your own beliefs:

    1. WANTING to change a belief.

    2. WILLING to change a belief.

You can educate someone on a tradition, explain where they come from and how you feel about them, but in most cases, you will need to step back and let the other person take their time to process the information and figure out how they feel about it. Do not force any of your own beliefs onto other people, or expect an immediate response; this will actually most likely achieve the opposite effect.

Be gentle with how you deliver information, and then give the person time to digest it and come to their own conclusion on the matter. If this means you do not end up influencing their belief, so be it; as long as everyone understands and respects each other's beliefs. People might need even more time than your engagement period to digest changes in traditions, and that is ok too; you have started the process, so well done.

3. ACCEPT CULTURAL DIFFERENCES AND SEE THE LIGHTER SIDE.

I recommend watching *My Big Fat Greek Wedding*. This comedy will show how you can make light of cultural bumps. No culture is more or less 'correct' than another, so encourage your family to be open and warm, and the rest will be beyond your control. Accept this. Anything that happens on your wedding day will make for funny memories in the future. In the moment, so long as it is not putting anyone in danger, all you can do is see the humour in any cultural misunderstandings. Make note though: laugh WITH the misunderstandings, not AT them. Laughter is the best medicine for cultural bumps!

4. YOU ARE NOT THE ONLY ONE WHO HAS BEEN DREAMING ABOUT YOUR WEDDING.

This day, your wedding day, is so much bigger than you and your partner. Your parents, your in-laws, your grandparents, have all been dreaming and looking forward to this day for you too. If you are like Luke and myself and are the first children to get married for each of your families, or the first grandchildren to get married, or even are moving to a different country post-wedding, this day can be particularly special and emotional for a lot of your family. Remember to think about other people's dreams, like maybe your father's dream of walking his daughter down the aisle. Your family's dreams are no less important than your own, so consider these when you are making your decision, and try and find a happy medium where everyone's dreams come true.

5. FIND SOMETHING OR SOMEONE TO UNLOAD ON.

Sometimes, a good rant will have to do in order to deal with any stubborn traditions. This could be a trusted person, a professional, or even a punching bag. You could even write a book like I have to help deal with them; this way you can comfort others and reassure them that they aren't alone. Any unexpected emotional outbursts in the heat of a discussion can potentially do more damage to a relationship, or to your chances of changing a tradition. Find that something or someone who you can confide in and let the steam come out that way instead.

6. IF YOU FEEL UNCOMFORTABLE, QUESTION IT.

If there is a tradition expected in your wedding that you feel uncomfortable about, don't be afraid to speak up. This can help wedding traditions evolve. You don't have to announce it at your family dinner; you can approach a person privately one-on-one if you feel more comfortable doing so, and go from there. Speak to family members who have been through it before, or speak to those who are key to any potential change in the tradition.

Note: It is completely normal to have a few uncomfortable or nervous feelings about getting married; it is a new chapter in your life and a big milestone. If you check out the sketch over the page, you will see that there are 2 rings around your comfort zone. The first ring is the stretch zone, and this is where the magic happens. This is where you can push your comfort zone a little bit and grow. The second outer ring is the panic zone. When you are sitting in this zone, you've been pushed too far out of your comfort zone and are, quite literally, panicking. These uncomfortable feelings are not good ones, and so you need to back up and try something different.

When it comes to getting married for the first time, it is normal for you to maybe be sitting in the stretch zone. There will be some uncomfortable feelings, some nerves, maybe some anxiety, but they are the good kind. You don't have to fight these if you feel in your gut, they are good for you.

If you're feeling that you're sitting in the panic zone, then speak up. This can be in regards to feelings about any detail, tradition or decision, and it very well could be about getting married. There could be a chance you felt pressured into getting married, and are sitting in the panic zone. Definitely speak to someone you trust if this is you. It could be any of the traditions I have spoken about in this chapter, or others that haven't been mentioned. Listen to your gut, and if you feel you are in the panic zone, speak up and ask questions.

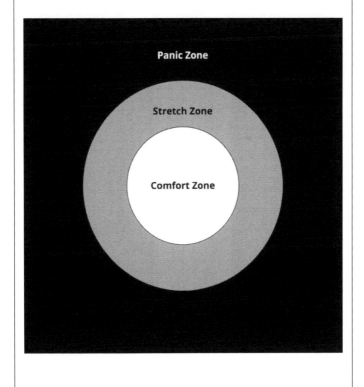

Summary of Questions in this Chapter

YOUR STORY BUILDING BLOCK #51: EQUAL ENGAGEMENT GIFTS

What do you think about both partners in the relationship getting an engagement ring/gift?
What does your partner think?
What have you chosen to do?

YOUR STORY BUILDING BLOCK #52: WHO IS PICKING THE RING DESIGN

Who is picking your engagement and wedding ring design?
What have you discussed with your partner?
If you're opting for your partner to choose the design, what specific requirements or guidelines do you wish to give your partner?
How do you and your partner feel about your final decision?

YOUR STORY BUILDING BLOCK #53: THE RING DESIGN ITSELF

If you haven't organised your engagement ring yet, what do you want for your engagement ring?
What do you want for your wedding ring?
What do you NOT want for your wedding ring? What design features don't you like?
Where can you look for inspiration?
How can you narrow your options down?
How do you want your ring and your partner's ring to match, if at all?

YOUR STORY BUILDING BLOCK #54: THE HAND YOU'LL BE WEARING YOUR RINGS ON

What hand will you wear your wedding ring on, if at all?

What hand will your partner be wearing their wedding ring on, if at all?

How do you feel about these decisions?

YOUR STORY BUILDING BLOCK #55: PASSING DOWN OF FAMILY RINGS

How do you feel about rings that are passed down in your family?

How open are your families in discussing this topic?

What other ways could you suggest to make the families happy but still end up with a ring that you are happy with?

Where does your partner sit on the issue?

When can you talk about this with your partner?

YOUR STORY BUILDING BLOCK #56: TRADITIONAL STEREOTYPES

How do you feel about gender-based traditional stereotypes?

What traditional stereotypes have you noticed during your wedding planning period?

What traditional stereotypes are you comfortable with?

What traditional stereotypes are you NOT comfortable with?

How do you want to handle situations when traditional stereotypes you don't agree with are brought up?

What might be some of the consequences of standing up to any traditional stereotypes you experience?

How comfortable are you in going against the grain and potentially standing out?

It's ok to accept a traditional stereotype for your wedding, even if you don't agree with it. This way, you don't have to compromise your beliefs. What traditional stereotypes are you content accepting as part of your wedding, but don't agree with?

YOUR STORY BUILDING BLOCK #57: WEDDING DAY OUTFIT CHOICE

What will you be wearing for your wedding day?

How many outfits will you be wanting/needing for your wedding day?

Who will you be taking with you to shop for your wedding day outfit, if anyone?

Who else gets a say in your wedding day outfit?

How open are they to different wedding day outfit styles?

How revealing is too revealing for you?

How revealing is too revealing for your parents/partner/grandparents?

What will happen if you and the people you are shopping with disagree on an outfit?

How will you resolve any disapprovals on your chosen wedding day outfit?

YOUR STORY BUILDING BLOCK #58: THE VEIL

What decision have you made with regards to a veil?

How do you feel about the veil?

How much say do you have in choosing this part of your wedding outfit?

Who else is this truly impacting?

YOUR STORY BUILDING BLOCK #59: THE GARTER AND BOUQUET THROW

How do you feel about the garter?

What decision have you made with regards to a garter?

What decision have you made with regards to the throwing of the bouquet?

What other games/activities would you like to have at your wedding instead, if any?

YOUR STORY BUILDING BLOCK #60: CULTURAL DIFFERENCES

What family clashes are you concerned about at your wedding?

What is in your control when it comes to these family clashes?

What is NOT in your control?

How similar are you and your partner's families?

How do they get along?

How can you change your perception on family culture clashes to make it more enjoyable for you on your wedding day?

YOUR STORY BUILDING BLOCK #61: RELIGIONS

What is you and your partner's religious situation?

How do you feel about your religious situation?

What extra religious factors do you need to consider?

What could you do to please your family and still be happy (i.e. a win-win scenario)?

YOUR STORY BUILDING BLOCK #62: WALKING DOWN THE AISLE

What are you choosing to do in regards to walking down the aisle?

Who is walking you down the aisle in your wedding?
How do you feel about this?
What options are available to you?
Who else do you need to consider in this decision?
How might they feel about this decision?
What can you do to come to a decision that all those involved agree on?

YOUR STORY BUILDING BLOCK #63: BRIDAL PARTY TRADITIONS

How many people make up your bridal party?
How do you feel about the group line-up?
What issues are you facing with your bridal party line-up?
What other bridal party ideas do you wish to do with your bridal party?
How are those closest to you accepting this?
What makes these decisions worth it?
How does your partner/parents/bridal party feel?
How best can you approach those who aren't accepting your bridal party decisions?

YOUR STORY BUILDING BLOCK #64: CHANGING UP THE SURNAME CHANGE

How open is your partner to discussing the surname change?
How progressive are you and your partner?
How supportive is your partner on your decision in regards to your surname?
How comfortable are you dealing with the thoughts of others on the matter?

YOUR STORY BUILDING BLOCK #65: ACCEPTED TRADITIONS

What traditions are unique to your family?

Which traditions are you happy following?

What traditions are you proud of?

What new family traditions do you wish to start?

What will you need to organise to start this tradition?

Further Reading on Traditions and Generation Gaps

- *The Rules of People* by Richard Templar

A repeat mention, but an easy-read book to understanding people and relations more. Key chapters relevant here are 'People Believe what they want to Believe', 'People are Tribal' and 'There's only one person you can change'.

- *White Weddings: Romancing Heterosexuality in Popular Culture* by Chrys Ingraham

One of the few books I found that looked into the culture around weddings. Almost a generation out of date now, but if you're interested in weddings as a research topic, this book would be a key one to include.

- Articles on same-sex weddings and traditions

Further study and research could go into weddings, both traditional and same-sex. There are many articles on the traditions of same-sex weddings and how they are being changed up, and here are a few that were used to inform this book:

  o For Australia: 'Same Sex Wedding Traditions We Love' by Roxanne at EasyWeddings.com [https://www.easyweddings.com.au/articles/same-sex-wedding-traditions-we-love/?fbclid=IwAR0Ba6Xm7ofqREx9C2GCQQop-i7NhDi4REqQ2eD5rzrF6aCIjwUe2gLrfJ0]

  o For UK: 'The New Same-Sex Marriage-Traditions' by Jonathon Wells for The Telegraph (2016) [https://www.telegraph.co.uk/family/relationships/the-new-same-sex-marriage-traditions/]

- **'My husband didn't take my last name' by Brita Long**
An interesting reversal of expectations on the surname change involved with marriage. You can find it here:
http://bellebrita.com/2015/02/husband-didnt-take-last-name/

Post-Wedding

We are coming towards the end now, so let's wrap your wedding up.

When people plan for their wedding, your mind does not normally go past the wedding day. Sure, there are some things that you can leave until after the wedding day to deal with. But, if by any chance, you have a little time for some early thought and preparation, future You will thank you.

You might also like to budget for post-wedding expenses. Giving the post-wedding items a little thought will help you avoid any unexpected costs.

For any wedding, as always, life is still going to be going on in the background. Maybe you are setting up a house to move into after your wedding; maybe you are pregnant and have a baby to prepare for; or maybe you are planning a honeymoon soon after the wedding. I count all these as post-wedding items, since they can't be forgotten and require your attention during the wedding lead up. These are common things that overlap with a wedding, so chances are you are planning for one of them in the background, or another that hasn't been mentioned. This means that all these events are probably mashed together in your brain, so this would not be a complete wedding planning book without giving them some attention!

Once the wedding has come and gone, you will feel a relief off your shoulders and may feel very ready to move on and close that chapter, as beautiful as your wedding was. However, this chapter will not be properly closed until all the loose ends are tied up, and because there typically isn't any urgency with these things, they can tend to drag on. Do yourself a favour and get onto these post-wedding items quick smart, so you can truly close the pages to this beautiful milestone in your life.

By now, you know the drill: firstly, empty your brain in the space below of all the memos, notes and things you need to remember for post-wedding, before we get into the chapter!

Your Story Brain Dump Space

My Story

As mentioned, it is highly likely that other life milestones will be occurring at the same time as your wedding. For us, we were moving to another country, and had to prepare for that. For other couples it has been building or renovating a new home together. For you it may well be something else. It is natural to see these events in a sequence—for example: wedding first, then move in, etc.—and prioritise them in that same order. It is easy to focus on the wedding, and forget that there's other big tasks to do at the same time. You can either feel the constant pressure of these tasks, or sit on them denying them attention while the wedding is first up on your priorities list. Because that's the reality of our thinking process sometimes: the wedding can seem like such a big milestone, that while the wedding is still in your future, the reality of the other milestones might not register. It's not until the wedding day comes and goes that your focus shifts and the next big thing becomes all too real.

To help you out, you can apply the timeline exercise described in the Practical Bits chapter. This timeline exercise can be applied to any other big project, so feel free to totally recycle it. To briefly summarise the process: first make a list of all the major items for your big project. Each of these items becomes a major marking post along your timeline towards your end goal: move-in date, baby's due date, etc. The second step is to work backwards to find dates for when each of the marking posts are needed to be completed by, and create a visual timeline. Once you have this timeline, cross-check it with the timeline you created for your wedding. See how you can arrange the marking posts on both timelines so that you can spread them all out, and avoid having a particularly intense period.

I'll use our London move to exemplify this: we first found out what were the major marking posts for the move—booking flights, visa application time allowances, passport steps—and created a timeline of when we needed to get everything done by. After we had our 'London move' timeline and our 'wedding' timeline, I overlapped them, and made sure that any big dates did not occur at the same time, so that I would not have something like 2 months of nothing and then 4 major marking posts due all at once. I would spread out my major marking posts so that, when there was a quiet period for the wedding planning, I would organise some documentation for the London move, etc., and vice versa. I also did this with my university degree, which was due to be completed this same year, ensuring nothing major was going on around exam time. However, when spreading out the major marking posts, keep in mind that you can bring them forward and complete them earlier, but pushing them back past their deadline dates will make them late.

YOUR STORY BUILDING BLOCK #66: MAJOR LIFE MILESTONES

Remind yourself: What are the major things going on in your life in the background of your wedding?
What are your priorities in life during this time?
How can you make sure everything is spread out so you don't have an intense period?
How do you wish to organise your milestones and identify overlapping busy periods?
What can you TRULY post-pone until after your wedding?

Another event, although not necessarily a milestone, is any day-after-the-wedding activities that you want to have. A lot of couples I know, including myself, have family barbeques or celebrations the day after the wedding. These aren't normally huge things, but because of how close they are to the wedding day, you're going to need to give attention to their preparation before your wedding day. This day is kind of like the calm after the storm, so is usually relaxed and a nice way to close off the wedding celebrations. Some people even choose to open all their wedding presents in front of close family and friends on this day. Still, items will need to be prepared (food, etc.), so a bit of time designated to this will be required.

YOUR STORY BUILDING BLOCK #67: THE DAY AFTER FAMILY EVENTS

What are you planning to do on the day after your wedding day?

What does your family want to do?

How much time will you need to devote to planning this day?

When can you put this into your schedule pre-wedding?

The above is for planning events that are coming up closely behind your wedding, but still require attention during the wedding planning period. Now we move on, the wedding day has occurred, and now to tie up all the leftover loose ends.

The first item I'm going to start with is any payments that need to be finalised post-wedding. Usually these are the last instalments for the bigger wedding items: the reception venue, photographers and videographers, etc. For example, we had the final instalment for our wedding venue due post-wedding because this payment depended on the final headcount. Our photographer and videographer were paid pre-wedding, but you may have the option to withhold the final payment until you have received the final product: the photos and the video. This can be a common thing with such services. These final instalments will probably be the first thing needed to be completed post-wedding, and will usually have a deadline. Any unpaid payments will most likely be chased, so you won't have to worry about forgetting them! Be a good customer and keep on top of them anyway. These will normally have been included in your wedding budget and accounted for, so there typically won't be any surprise payments here, unless major damage was caused at your wedding, in which case you may have incurred extra costs.

YOUR STORY BUILDING BLOCK #68: FINAL PAYMENTS POST-WEDDING
> **What final payments will you have?**
> **When do you have to pay them by?**

The other side of the equation is collecting any bonds paid. Bonds are the security payments you put down with your florist, equipment hire, etc. in case any equipment that belongs to them that you are borrowing for the day gets damaged. If it is not damaged, then great, you can return and get your money back. If it is damaged, well, no, you don't get your money back. Something we noticed in the little fine print of our invoice from our florist, is that if we returned the big cardboard boxes that our bouquets had been delivered in, we got an extra bond back too. A cardboard box! Normally we would've just folded this up and thrown it in the recycling bin. It is worth checking what little bits you can return and get some more money back from, which can top up the wedding pot. Keep all the paperwork from the vendors and suppliers, and return equipment as soon as possible after the wedding. You don't want these bits hanging around the house, potentially increasing the risk of damage and dust, and sticking around on your to-do list.

YOUR STORY BUILDING BLOCK #69: MONEY-BACK OPTIONS POST-WEDDING

What bonds can you get back after the wedding? (Check your answer to the same question in Building Block #41!)

How can you remind yourself to act on these post-wedding?

Who can you check with for items you're unsure about?

When will you be able to do this post-wedding? Set a date.

The next post-wedding task to do will be the cleaning of your wedding garments. Whatever you do with your wedding dress/outfit—whether you sell it, store it, donate it—you're going to probably clean it first. This is not the cheapest thing to do. Some bridal shops include this in with the purchase of a wedding dress, and it might just be a case of bringing the dress into the store and they will organise it to be professionally cleaned. But this all depends on where you get your dress from. Not all places will provide this service (especially non-bridal shops), so you might need to open the wedding wallet again. You might want to include this in your wedding budget; that way you have accounted for it and aren't shocked with the extra cost post-wedding. After all, it's usually the costs that we least expect and have not planned for that frustrate us the most. This also goes for the suits and maybe the bridesmaids' dresses, especially if you hired them. Again, hire shops might happily accept them dirty because they organise the cleaning themselves; others might not. There is no common way here, so do a little questioning to get your answers on what to do. If you own the garment, then you will have to pay for the cleaning yourself. The sooner you get these done after the wedding the better; you don't want clothes hanging around with smells and dirt in them. Sometimes, the longer they sit dirty, the harder they are to clean. Plus, the longer you leave it, the more you accept that leaving it is ok, and the less likely you are to ever get them cleaned, even though they will still be in the back of your mind. Get it done at your earliest convenience, so you can wipe your hands of this wedding chapter in your life and move on with your marriage.

YOUR STORY BUILDING BLOCK #70: WEDDING GARMENTS

What are you going to do with your wedding dress/outfit post-wedding?
When will you be getting any wedding garments cleaned?
When will you be returning any hired garments?
How much are the cleaning services going to cost?
Who can you speak to about recommended cleaning services for special wedding garments?

Another thing you do not want hanging around is your wedding gift money. That is a decent chunk of cash if you received only monetary gifts. That is all gift money, therefore no paper trail exists, and if you lose it or if it gets stolen, there is not much you can do. Sounds unlikely, but it is not impossible. If you don't want to put it into a bank, and have another purpose for it, no worries, just be careful if it's a big sum. We put our wedding gift money into a bank account as soon as possible. Luke and I had been living pretty separate lives up until we got married, and we didn't have a bank account together yet. We organised one straight after the wedding and deposited our money into it. We needed to bring in our marriage certificate to prove that all the cash was a result of our recent wedding, so do think about this if this is the route you decide to go. If you already have an account that you will be depositing your money into, great. If not, you may want to set it up prior to the wedding in preparation. This is one of those tasks that could definitely be left until post-wedding, as opening an account doesn't take too long. Just have a chat to clarify what you and your partner want to do.

YOUR STORY BUILDING BLOCK #71: WEDDING GIFT MONEY

What are you going to do with your wedding gift money?

Where are you going to store it?

What will you need to organise in preparation for this storage?

When will you be able to organise this? Set a date.

If you were able to receive any free services, donations or help from people throughout your friends and family, you might be wanting to organise some thank you gifts. You may particularly like to give thank you gifts to your parents, especially if they were paying for your wedding or helped you out in other big ways. We started organising these gifts *before* the wedding, because we didn't have much time after the wedding before we moved overseas. We organised a basket of all kinds of goodies for each of our parents. TIP: For any kind of gift that has a lot of pieces to it, start them nice and early, so whenever you have a random idea, or find something that would be great for the gift, you can add it in, there and then. Over time, you will slowly fill the basket, to the point that it is ready to go. For a gift like this, with lots of parts, it can be harder to set out one day to buy a whole bunch of items; you either can't find what you're looking for, don't know what you want to get, or feel rushed because it got left too late.

You may also like to organise thank you gifts for your bridal party. We didn't buy specific gifts for ours, but we did give them everything they needed for the wedding, which they got to keep. As well as the suits and dresses, Luke bought his groomsmen tie pins and cufflinks with each of their initials on them, as well as their shoes and belts, and I wrote thank you cards for all my bridesmaids to go along with their earrings and bracelets, shoes, clutch purses filled with their own mini 'Wedding Day Survival Kit', as well as a small gift of goodies I had given them earlier in the year. These were essentially their thank you gifts and tokens of appreciation from Luke and I. If you're supplying everything for your bridal party, this may be an option you'd like to consider too.

YOUR STORY BUILDING BLOCK #72: THANK YOU GIFTS

How do you feel about thank you gifts?
Who do you wish to give thank you gifts to?
How much do you want to spend on thank you gifts?
What are you going to give as thank you gifts?
How do you wish to organise these?
When do you want to organise these?

One of the most common traditions for after a wedding is the honeymoon. I spoke earlier about a pre-wedding honeymoon if you can, but boy do you need a post-wedding one. Just like the pre-honeymoon, it doesn't need to be extravagant. It can literally be just a couple of days home from work that you get to spend with your new husband or wife. Or, on the other end of the scale, it can definitely be a big holiday. I know of couples who have had up to six months for their honeymoon. But, if you are having a big holiday, make yourself aware of any holiday planning you might need to do *before* the wedding day. This might be one of those overlapping events. You may wish to have a honeymoon months after your wedding. There are lots of advantages to doing so: financially you can let your pocket recoup a bit, and save up some money for your honeymoon, or you might just like to spread the events out. Sometimes when you have a wedding followed by a big holiday, one straight after the other, they can feel rushed or over in a flash, so spreading them out can help you enjoy them more. In which case, maybe you choose both options: have those few days alone together initially straight after your wedding, and then plan a bigger holiday later. It is all totally up to you.

Whatever your situation, a few days together alone at the very minimum is NEEDED. A honeymoon is not *just* a holiday like I had initially thought all those months ago. It is a break to relax and catch up with yourself, spend quality time as a newlywed couple, and reflect on the hopefully good time that was your wedding.

YOUR STORY BUILDING BLOCK #73: HONEYMOON
What do you want to do for your honeymoon?
Where do you want to go for your honeymoon?
How long can you go for?
When are you going to go?

How can you ensure you have at least a few days together and alone with your partner post-wedding?

Once all is said and done, and you are winding down into your new married life, it is easy to leave the wedding behind and get on with your career, maybe your new house, etc. Then months later, you suddenly recall that you never received your wedding photos! Your wedding photos, and wedding video if you had one, can take months after your wedding to finally arrive on your doorstep. They can very easily be forgotten. If you have hired a professional, they can be trusted to let you know when they are done, and inform you on the process. They will usually also give you a rough date as to when your wedding photos or video will be ready. But you still might like to keep a tab on these guys and touch base to see how things are going. You may need to keep in touch to finalise details, or make decisions on photos, etc. For us, this was super delayed because we were in London. Fortunately, all was good, but because so much time had lapsed, some of the details of our photo package had been forgotten, so it proved to be really important that we had our original paperwork still. The forgotten details were remedied straight away; it was just an honest mistake due to how much time had passed. What was very helpful was keeping all that paperwork, so don't ditch it too hastily post-wedding. Usually wedding photos and videos are not cheap, so this isn't one you want to forget.

YOUR STORY BUILDING BLOCK #74: WEDDING PHOTOS AND VIDEOS
   What are the details of your wedding photos or video package?
   When will they be ready by?

How can you remind yourself of these products?
How will you keep in touch with your photographer/videographer?
How can you ensure you keep the paperwork in a safe and memorable place?

Lastly, there's the paperwork for your surname change, if you are changing it. If you aren't planning on changing any names, then you won't need to worry about this. But if you are, then you will have a little paperwork to fill out. It usually is a matter of organising a copy of the legal marriage certificate (not the one issued by a religious house), and making an appointment with the appropriate body to change your passport details.

I personally avoided this straight after the wedding for 2 reasons:

1. Because we were moving to London so soon after the wedding, I didn't want to risk not having my passport in time.

2. Because I didn't know what I wanted to do with my surname change yet and didn't want to rush the decision.

If one or both of you are wanting to change your surname, don't feel like you have to legally do it straight away, post-wedding. People can call you whatever you want them to, on social media, etc., but legally there is no rush. I waited a year and a half after my wedding to organise the change. That is when I felt ready. It really is a bizarre feeling to change your name, so please, please, please, do not feel pressured into doing it straight away. And don't stress: if you change your surname, regret it and want to change it back, technically you can. Depending on the country you live in, there might be a limit to how many times you can change your name, but it's still doable. Keep in mind, it is your *name*, and you don't want to be changing it too many times, so choose to wait until you feel ready rather than rush into it and potentially regret it. If your partner is upset at your lack of urgency to change your name, try explaining to them how it is making you feel and how you just want to take your time for such a big step. It is just something you need time to process and get used to. You could ask them to imagine the roles were reversed, and that it was them who had to change their name, their NAME, and see how they would feel doing that overnight. Hopefully they will understand. If they don't, that's unfortunate, but you will not be able to control their thinking process. This might be one of those things you have to agree to disagree on with your partner, and still attempt the change at your own pace. You may be happy with the urgency to change your name, and you may be happy to change it even if you don't feel ready. You might think, whether you change it now or later, it's going to change regardless, so let's get this over with. It is totally up to you.

YOUR STORY B*UILDING* B*LOCK* #75: *SURNAME CHANGE ADMIN*

> *Remind yourself of your answer to this question from Building Block #23: How much time will you take to change your surname post-wedding?*
>
> *When are you going to organise the appropriate documentation and appointment?*
>
> *What does your partner think about this?*
>
> *How will your partner's thoughts affect your decision on when you will be changing your surname?*
>
> *How will this affect your relationship with your partner?*

Suggestion Box

1. SET TIME ASIDE EARLY TO PLAN ALL THE BIG THINGS GOING ON IN YOUR LIFE.

If you have a couple of big life milestones happening at the same time as your wedding, then sit down early in your engagement and set out a timeline of events. If you can spread out major marking posts so that you don't have a lot of stuff happening at the same time, this will help reduce panic and stress. If you like a busy life pace, then go nuts. But if you don't, then plan it early and spread it out.

2. MAKE A LIST OF ALL THE BONDS AND MONEY-BACK ITEMS AVAILABLE TO YOU.

As you plan your wedding and go through the process, you may be told or read in an invoice or contract of potential money-back opportunities if you return some equipment in good condition. Add these items to a list so you don't forget post-wedding. Keep this list in a safe place (maybe altogether with your other wedding paperwork if you have adopted the suggestions from chapter Practical Bits), and pull it out the night before the wedding to check what items need to be taken care of and not thrown away the next day. Pull this list out again post-wedding so you can work through it, tick things off as you return them and collect your money back. Check that the bonds don't have an expiry date, where if passed, you can't get your bond back.

3. RETURN HIRED GOODS AND ORGANISE GARMENT CLEANING AS SOON AS POSSIBLE.

Similarly, from point no. 2, there may be dates which, if passed, you might incur a fee for returning hired goods late. To avoid this, return everything hired as soon as possible after your wedding. Same goes for cleaning—I recommend getting those dresses, suits, etc. cleaned as soon as possible. You don't want these items hanging around your house and on your to-do list. You want to move on from this wedding chapter and get on with married life. These are the final parts to close the wedding and as sad as that may make you feel, get these bits and pieces done, and then you can just look forward to receiving the wedding photos!

4. KEEP IN CONTACT WITH YOUR PHOTOGRAPHER AND VIDEOGRAPHER.

The wedding photos and video (if you engaged in these services) usually take a long time to come through. This is fine —just don't forget what you ordered. Have everything written down. From our experience, it is worth keeping in touch with your photographer and/or videographer and making sure you are happy with everything. Don't lose contact with them if you haven't received everything you ordered. This can easily happen when your wedding was months ago and you have already gotten into the swing of normality again. You probably won't even be thinking about your wedding anymore. So put dates and reminders in your diaries, because these services are not cheap and you don't want to be forgetting them.

5. DEPOSIT WEDDING GIFT MONEY AS SOON AS POSSIBLE.

People normally store lumps of cash in a bank, so I'm guessing it's a safe bet you're most likely going to store your wedding gift money in a bank account too. You don't have to, but just be careful with a huge lump of cash that does not have a paper trail of existence. I recommend depositing your wedding gift money as soon after your wedding as possible. If you already have the account you want to put the money into set up already, you are one step ahead.

6. KEEP ALL YOUR WEDDING PAPERWORK.

You might feel like throwing it all away once the wedding is done, but it's actually worth keeping. It can be easy to forget the details of the wedding packages you invested in months ago, so the paperwork can be very useful for finalising the bill and ensuring everything you initially paid for is present.

The paperwork for our wedding has also come in handy for reference for planning our sibling's wedding and a cousin's wedding, so it may actually be useful for someone else too!

Summary of Questions in this Chapter

YOUR STORY BUILDING BLOCK #66: MAJOR LIFE MILESTONES

Remind yourself: What are the major things going on in your life in the background of your wedding?

What are your priorities in life during this time?

How can you make sure everything is spread out so you don't have an intense period?

How do you wish to organise your milestones and identify overlapping busy periods?

What can you TRULY post-pone until after your wedding?

YOUR STORY BUILDING BLOCK #67: THE DAY AFTER FAMILY EVENTS

What are you planning to do on the day after your wedding day?

What does your family want to do?

How much time will you need to devote to planning this day?

When can you put this into your schedule pre-wedding?

YOUR STORY BUILDING BLOCK #68: FINAL PAYMENTS POST-WEDDING

What final payments will you have?

When do you have to pay them by?

YOUR STORY BUILDING BLOCK #69: MONEY-BACK OPTIONS POST-WEDDING

What bonds can you get back after the wedding? (Check your answer to the same question in Building

Block #41!)

How can you remind yourself to act on these post-wedding?

Who can you check with for items you're unsure about?

When will you be able to do this post-wedding? Set a date.

YOUR STORY BUILDING BLOCK #70: WEDDING GARMENTS

What are you going to do with your wedding dress/outfit post-wedding?

When will you be getting any wedding garments cleaned?

When will you be returning any hired garments?

How much are the cleaning services going to cost?

Who can you speak to about recommended cleaning services for special wedding garments?

YOUR STORY BUILDING BLOCK #71: WEDDING GIFT MONEY

What are you going to do with your wedding gift money?

Where are you going to store it?

What will you need to organise in preparation for this storage?

When will you be able to organise this? Set a date.

YOUR STORY BUILDING BLOCK #72: THANK YOU GIFTS

How do you feel about thank you gifts?

Who do you wish to give thank you gifts to?

How much do you want to spend on thank you gifts?

What are you going to give as thank you gifts?
How do you wish to organise these?
When do you want to organise these?

YOUR STORY BUILDING BLOCK #73: HONEYMOON

What do you want to do for your honeymoon?
Where do you want to go for your honeymoon?
How long can you go for?
When are you going to go?
How can you ensure you have at least a few days together and alone with your partner post-wedding?

YOUR STORY BUILDING BLOCK #74: WEDDING PHOTOS AND VIDEOS

What are the details of your wedding photos or video package?
When will they be ready by?
How can you remind yourself of these products?
How will you keep in touch with your photographer/videographer?
How can you ensure you keep the paperwork in a safe and memorable place?

YOUR STORY BUILDING BLOCK #75: SURNAME CHANGE ADMIN

Remind yourself of your answer to this question from Building Block #23: How much time will you take to change your surname post-wedding?
When are you going to organise the appropriate documentation and appointment?
What does your partner think about this?

How will your partner's thoughts affect your decision on when you will be changing your surname?

How will this affect your relationship with your partner?

Conclusion

I feel like I have just relived my wedding experience. All the wedding feels came flooding back. It was such a full-on time in my life, and both Luke and I achieved so much that year. I have no doubt it will be a huge time for you as well.

After all the tears, the excitement, the anxiety and all the joy, it really was an exhausting year. I gave this book to my mum to read while I was writing it, and after all we went through that year, she turned around to me and said she had not remembered any of the drama. I quote her words: "All I remember is the beautiful day you and Luke had".

That sort of sums it up really. Despite all the detail I have gone into about our wedding planning journey leading up to the big day, I agree with my mum, as that is how I remember the day as well: the beautiful day Luke and I had. All the emotions and hard work leading up to the day was worth it. When I think about our wedding, all I can think of is Luke's face. Luke is the kind of person who wears his feelings on his sleeve: he can't hide anything. The way he looked at me on our wedding day, sums up all my feelings that day. The way he looked at me made absolutely everything worth it. And, to this day, the broken party favours and the wedding stresses don't matter anymore, what matters is that Luke still looks at me in the same way, and I at him. That is what truly matters when it comes to a wedding: it is the start of your marriage. Maybe that is why some people describe their wedding as the best day of their life; not for the day itself, but for how it represents the start of your marriage. And for me, every day since has been an absolute blessing of a marriage.

Food for thought for you: it occurred to me recently that it takes longer to plan a wedding than it does to make a baby. And making a baby is pretty impressive. I would not call that an easy task at all for the woman who has to carry the baby for 9 months. But it takes longer to plan a wedding... what does that say about planning a wedding? I haven't had a baby yet, so I can't really answer that question. But an interesting thought... one for another book perhaps.

Ok, let's sum up the journey we have been through in this book. A wedding is, at the very foundation, a big event that you need to plan, so we started with the practical bits of a wedding. I showed you how you can create a plan for your wedding, both a simple one and a complex one, and then how to organise the major parts into marking posts along a timeline. This timeline can be used as a guide to what tasks to tackle first. I talked through how you can prioritise your tasks, and create order in your plan of action. This was the first chapter as creating a plan is one of the first things you can do when setting out on your wedding planning journey. This will help minimise any overwhelm that could be potentially caused by lack of organisation.

The next big part of the wedding planning, which comes into every single part, is communication. I talked about defining who you will be communicating with, strategies you can use to keep communications clear and simple to make sure everyone is understood, and how it is ok to agree to disagree on different opinions. I also shared some of the communication tools I prepared for the wedding day that you can use too. These can help you communicate with people without physically being in the equation and, in doing so, allowing yourself to focus on simply enjoying your wedding day.

We then moved onto some of the more sensitive areas that are involved in a wedding, starting with mental health. I found that, in a heterosexual couple, there is more pressure on the bride than on the groom, and mentally this can weigh you down if you are conscious of these gender roles. I spoke about what I found hard to mentally deal with and, if you experience something similar, how you can work through these. This is also a time that you might want to ramp up the self-care, including spending quality time alone with your partner. These times can help you get through some of the tougher days, and give you treats to look forward to.

I arranged the mental health chapter before the money chapter because of its importance, but finances can be a big cause of stress and anxiety when it comes to a wedding. I find that it is a sense of lack of control over money that can cause you the most stress, so I talked about how you can utilise money management tools such as Excel, keep your spreadsheets clear and organised, and keep them constantly updated. This helps not only as your wedding budget, but also as a communicating tool between your partner, parents and anyone else contributing to your wedding costs. I shared a few examples of how you can reduce your wedding costs, as well as provided you with the super spreadsheet template that I used for our wedding.

The next 2 sections were sensitive because we started talking about the family. Your wedding might be more of a family affair than you initially realise, so family politics might be something you'll need to navigate through regularly. Our wedding was relatively smooth because our families are so similar, but yours might not be. There can be a few bumps in the road, and this is to be expected because everyone is different and thinks differently. I shared some of the key areas where family politics are likely to come up, such as the guest list, seating arrangements and wedding speeches, as well as touching on disagreements again and your family communications.

A lot of family politics derives from differences in opinions on traditions, so the chapter on wedding traditions and generation gaps followed. As the youngest generation, you're naturally probably going to have more modern ideas than your parents or grandparents, so this can create a few traditional clashes. We had a few in our wedding planning experience, most of them derived from traditional heterosexual gender roles that didn't sit well with my 21st Century values. Other traditions can be cultural or religious. How to work through your tradition clashes is up to you, but hopefully this chapter reassured you that you are not alone in your experience, and gave you a few ideas as to how to work with them. Whilst I mostly spoke about traditions that you might not agree with, there will be others that you'll want to embrace, or even create yourself.

Lastly, we finished with the lightest of the chapters, the post-wedding chapter. This chapter describes all the wedding-related tasks that happen AFTER the wedding. Before the wedding there is so much physical and emotional preparation for the day itself, that it is easy to not want to give any thought to the post-wedding tasks until after the wedding. I discussed the post-wedding items that you might need to address, and potentially even devote some time pre-wedding to prepare for.

The sooner these are done, the sooner you can close your wedding chapter and start enjoying and settling into your new married life.

In each of the chapters there has been a box of suggestions for your wedding, based on my experience. Throughout the My Story sections, there are 75 building blocks of choice coaching-style questions to help you build YOUR story, and think about different aspects of your wedding planning. The chapters all finish with a summary of these questions, so you don't have to go fishing through the pages to find them again; just shoot straight to the end of the relevant chapter.

The primary goal for sharing my wedding story with you in this book has been to exemplify what planning for a wedding can actually look like. As far as I can find, this hasn't been done before, and knowing someone else's story in such detail can help you to know what to expect for your own wedding planning journey. In an ideal world, my bigger picture goal is that I would love if this book ignites some research into weddings, and for more personal stories out there to come out about traditions, gender roles, and their impacts.

In the mental health chapter, I suggested having someone who you can unload on. This can be a trusted friend or family member, but you might find this difficult—as I initially did—because, if they are close enough to talk to, they are probably involved in the wedding and therefore sensitive to what you are saying. If you prefer to engage with someone removed from the wedding, you might seek a professional to confide in during this wedding planning time. If you are less concerned about just unloading and more concerned with finding solutions, working out how to deal with certain hurdles that come your way, and creating an action plan for your wedding, you might like to consider a life coach. If this is you, and you have found this book helpful, check out my website www.letsgetyourlifetogether.com/bridalcoaching for information on performance coaching with me. This book has been written to help as many brides-to-be as possible, but it's not tailored to the individual, which is what coaching with me will provide. We will work with your wedding and your feelings without any judgement, and help you work towards having the best wedding planning experience possible for you and your partner.

I hope you have been able to take something away from this book. I have written it all with love, but everyone's wedding experience is going to be different, and you may or may not find familiarity in parts of my story. The more I travel, and the more I meet new people, the more I find that we are actually more similar than we think. Even if you don't agree with some of the items I've shared, you might recognise similarities with other issues you are experiencing. Even if you aren't facing the same stresses and anxieties that I faced, you may feel stressed and anxious about other details. I am confident that most families will have some form of family politics, and thus will benefit from improved communications. All weddings will have to be paid for, and all weddings will need at least a little bit of planning. So hopefully you can walk away, just a little bit more confident in your abilities to plan your wedding, with a few more tools in your belt, and a couple of new ideas. It is a time in your life that doesn't come along very often, so let's keep it special, but let's also keep it real. So much time, money, and preparation go into just one day. Everyone always makes out the wedding day to be the special day, but in reality, it's the wedding planning journey that counts for so much more. So, enjoy and take care to make the journey special too.

To you, and all the other brides-to-be reading this book, I wish you all the very best with your wedding planning. I hope it is a beautiful and fun period in your life for you and your partner, and that you use this moment in time to also learn something about yourself. All the hard work you are probably doing right now will pay off, and by the wedding day it will all come together. After all the hard work, I myself was surprisingly calm on my wedding day; I wish for you the same peace on yours.

And if anything does not go to plan on the day, smile, shrug and choose to laugh it off!

Appendix A: TIPS

TIP: Speak to your own caterers to see how much notice they require, and then add another week on for chasing up to figure out the RSVP date for your invitations.

TIP: Even if your marriage documentation doesn't have to be filled out and submitted for a long time, ensure you know what you need to fill out early, and the dates it needs to be submitted by.

TIP: Ordering some food for the morning of is something you might like to think about for your wedding day. On such a big day, eating can be the first thing you forget to do, so this will ensure you are not running on an empty stomach!

TIP: If you do create a schedule, add some buffer time to each activity. For example, did the make-up lady say she can do a face in 30 minutes? Then allow 40-45 minutes. Adding that extra 5-15 minutes to each timeslot will take the pressure off, and it will feel better when you start finishing up early, according to the schedule. It will also allow time for toilet breaks, spontaneous phone calls, or snack breaks.

TIP: For your wedding photoshoots, make a list of the order of the photos, like this:

1. Photo #1: Luke and Juliet
2. Photo #2: Luke, Juliet, and Luke's parents
3. Photo #3: Luke, Juliet, and Juliet's parents
4. Photo #4: Luke, Juliet, and siblings
5. …
6. …

Designate someone as the photo organiser and give them this list. They can then organise who is needed for each photo and get the people for the next photo ready to go, especially if you're on a tight schedule.

TIP: Speak to your wedding vendors and suppliers, as they know from experience what has and hasn't worked well in past weddings they have been part of, and may have a few tricks up their sleeves to help you with your wedding.

TIP: Print off spares of any lists, schedules, etc. that you require for your wedding day.

TIP: When you are in a conversation with someone who is probing too far for your liking, I found simply making it a humorous game made them go away: "You will have to wait and see!" Sticking to this response stubbornly made the probers laugh and go away. Rarely do people argue with this response.

TIP: Communicate to the people closest to you what *kind* of support you need at any given time.

TIP: If you can have your wedding at a hotel venue, there are some great advantages. As well as being able to stay put and not worry about transport at the end of your wedding, another added bonus of having your wedding reception in a hotel was you and your bridal party can head to your rooms before the reception, take your shoes off, have a few drinks and freshen up. We got to do this, and it was particularly great since it was a hot day and boy did we need a few drinks! This way, the whole bridal party got a chance to breathe and enjoy the moment too. You do not want to rush through your wedding day and miss these moments to soak everything up and just enjoy!

TIP: For your overall budget—if it is possible for you—add a bit of money on top, just to give you a buffer. This could be anywhere from rounding budgets to the nearest ten, to adding a few thousand on top. This can give you a little trick of the mind: it will feel better to over-budget and come under, then to under-budget and go over! Do be careful though if you think this won't work for you; some people will see the buffer as just more room for more. But I know that for us this worked well, and it may also suit you too.

TIP: Make any task as easy as possible to do in order to maintain it.

TIP: If given the choice, opt for payments in instalments. This will help minimise financial pressure wherever possible, and spread out the spending.

TIP: For anyone who is in a similar situation, send out a spreadsheet to your wedding payers via email regularly so that everyone can look through it at their own pace. Make it as easy as possible for everyone to work with you, so that your wedding payers feel at their most comfortable with your money management.

TIP: Re-use any decorations you've used for previous parties. These tend to get shoved in spare rooms or sheds, but give them a new lease of life and re-use them for small wedding bits.

TIP: Pinterest can be your best friend during your wedding planning months; I got so many amazing and beautiful wedding ideas, but also creative and cheap ideas as well.

TIP: The part of the bridesmaids' dresses that had the biggest influence on whether we required alterations or not was the dress length. My bridesmaids' dresses were calf-length, so none of them needed alterations. If the dresses were to the floor dresses, they definitely would have needed hemming as most dresses are longer than required for mass production. So, if you wish to cut costs or avoid extra tasks, consider the dress length for this. It will just be a matter of ordering the correct sizes.

TIP: Ensure the font type and font size on your invitations is big and clear enough to be read easily.

TIP: If you have had other parties in your recent past—birthday parties, etc.—where you can recycle the guest lists for your wedding guest list, do so. This will give you a head start and more importantly a starting point that you can move forward with.

TIP: For any kind of gift that has a lot of pieces to it, start them nice and early, so whenever you have a random idea, or find something that would be great for the gift, you can add it in, there and then. Over time, you will slowly fill the gift, to the point that it is ready to go. For a gift like this, with lots of parts, it can be harder to set out one day to buy a whole bunch of items; you either can't find what you're looking for, don't know what you want to get, or feel rushed because it got left too late.